To get Ozmabee
With best wishes
Joe H Strow

JOE STROUD

Free Press Sunday Morning

Detroit Free Press

Editor: Gerald Skora
Art direction and production: Andrew J. Hartley
Copyediting: Patricia C. Foley
Cover photograph: Tony Spina
Special assistance: Linda McCraith

Printed in U.S.A. on recycled paper

ISBN 0-937247-52-9

To Lee Hills, who gave me this forum

To have this forum has been and is a very special privilege. I have had as much freedom and as much autonomy as any other editor in America, I suspect. That is an extraordinary gift to a kid from Arkansas who used to seek solitude in the top of the hay barn just to play around with words and ideas. I count myself lucky to have had such a forum for a single day.

— JOE STROUD,
Nov. 26, 1989

Contents

The City: From Billy Rogell to Coleman Young

The State: From Pigeon River to Lafayette Clinic

The Nation: From Vietnam to Reaganomics

The World: From Anwar Sadat to Saddam Hussein

Race: From Orval Faubus to Nelson Mandela

The Press: From Spiro Agnew to the JOA

Family: From Mom on the Farm to Children in the City

Introduction

The columns contained in this collection represent 25 years of Joe Stroud's life as a journalist for the Detroit Free Press; 25 years of reflecting thoughtfully on the spiritual strength of this community and its people; 25 years of bringing readers a message of hope, of promise, of better times to come.

They also represent 25 years of making sure all who read him understand that without justice there can be no hope, without equality there are only promises unfulfilled, and without commitment there will be no better times. If those with the direct responsibility to deliver justice, hope, equality and better times fail in that responsibility, they can be assured that Joe Stroud will insist on an accounting from them.

This, of course, creates the problem of bringing messages that are not always happy ones, something that tends to place an uncommon burden on the messenger. Those who hold a mirror to communities such as Detroit are often blamed for what the community sees of itself.

There are, of course, choices for these messengers. They can wallow in the hopelessness of it all and blame the most convenient villain, offering no hope, no solutions.

Or, like Joe Stroud, they can deal directly with the problems that shadow all of urban America and talk about what needs to be done — and by whom — to make this a better place for all of us to work, live and raise our families.

There's an aphorism that suggests that nothing contributes more to peace of soul than having no opinion at all.

If that, indeed, is the price for a peaceful soul, it has no currency on the editorial pages over which Joe Stroud presides.

— *Neal Shine, Publisher of the Detroit Free Press*

THE CITY

From Billy Rogell to Coleman Young

CHAPTER ONE

'Why don't people understand ... ?'

She was barely 10, and the city had, till then, been no more than a distant abstraction, an alabaster place undimmed by human tears.

But this city was her city now, and with her family, she was seeing it for the first time.

Maybe we should all see it for the first time.

It began, this primer course in urban sociology, on the tree-shaded northwest side. She knew and understood that kind of place, with its quiet streets that could be set down intact in a thousand other American cities and still be home.

Outside, the first new notion that came to her was the scale of things.

"Why," she wanted to know, "does it take so long to get places?"

Traffic and people and lights and automobiles, she was told.

And then, as Grand River Avenue went past her window, she saw something else new. "Why," she demanded to know, "are so many stores boarded up?"

AUG. 12, 1968

It is not easy to rebuild cities and to remember that people don't want to be pushed around and that somehow, with renewal, there must also be stability.

The riot. The natural decay of buildings no longer desirable. The carelessness of past planning.

"Did they have a riot here, too?" she said, forgetting last summer's impressions from afar.

The worst in recent American history. She fell thoughtfully silent for a while.

"Why don't they tear this down?" she wanted to know after an interlude. And looking beyond the row of decrepit buildings to the still-tree-lined streets behind, she added, "It could be so much prettier if all these old buildings were torn away."

That, she was told, is urban renewal. But urban renewal takes time and costs money, and it has often been misused, and the city cannot be renewed fast enough.

From there the family drove across downtown to Lafayette Park and Elmwood I.

Here, she was told, is some of what urban renewal had done.

It looked nice, she thought.

But then there were the fringes of Elmwood, with more of the broken houses, the tired, neglected houses in the area due to be cleared.

"How many of these people," the mother asked, "can move back into the renewal area?"

Not many can afford to, and that is the tragedy. And so often we have forgotten to worry enough about those who move from the bulldozer's path.

"Why," said the 10-year-old again, "why don't people understand that it's hard to leave home, even a crummy home?"

A lot of mistakes have been made, she was told; it is not easy to rebuild cities and to remember that people don't want to be pushed around and that somehow, with renewal, there must also be stability.

At this, she lapsed again into the silence of one who is shocked at the real world she finds beyond the land of her dreams.

Finally, she had another question or two about abandoned buildings and children at play around them and why more and better things could not be done.

There was another moment of silence, and then a flash of honest, little-girl anger.

"I don't know why people can't be helped more. I bet I could figure out a better way in five minutes than the cities have now."

Maybe so, little 10-year-old. Maybe so. Or maybe you, like the rest of us, will lose your way somewhere between what we see is wrong with our cities and what we can do about it.

Young's inauguration revives a dream

As Detroit has moved toward and through this Inaugural Week, the theme that has been running through my head has been a passage from Dr. Martin Luther King's speech at the climax of the 1963 March on Washington.

"I have a dream," he said, "that one day on the red hills of Georgia the sons of former slaves and the sons of former slave owners will be able to sit down together at the table of brotherhood … I have a dream that one day every valley shall be exalted, every hill and mountain shall be made low. The rough places will be made plains, and the crooked places will be made straight. And the glory of the Lord shall be revealed, and all flesh shall see it together. This is our hope."

To be sure, Detroit is not "the red hills of Georgia," but the struggle for a just and open society has, in the years since Dr. King's death, been concentrated more in the big cities of the industrial states than in the rural South. And the dream has seemed as often threatened by what happened in the cities.

JAN. 4, 1974

If Coleman Young is a good leader, he has a chance such as no one else has ever had to bank the fires of racial hate, to make Detroit more a dream and less a nightmare.

Dreams, of course, aren't enough to build cities, or overcome racial divisions, or make our town a place of hope rather than a place of fear.

Indeed, one of Detroit's troubles has been that it was a place where men came seeking dreams and wound up with nightmares — nightmares of unemployment, of crime, of hostility, of disillusionment. For many people in rural America, particularly the rural South, Detroit was a symbol of a hope for a better life, but when they came, many were disappointed, or angry and bitter.

There have been many reasons for such disillusionment. The one-industry character of the economy has made the area susceptible to the gyrations of the business cycle. The clash of the cultures of those who came from the rural South and those who came from Europe has often been harsh and marred by periodic explosions.

Even the climate itself has served to aggravate the suffering of the poor. The industrial leadership too early and for too long turned its back on the central city, and the unions often confused their own narrow and selfish interests with the public interest.

But Detroit's central problem has been the problem of race: The distrust and fear of white for black and black for white, aggravated by two of the worst riots in American history, fed by the facts and rumors of everyday life.

The problem is not unique to Detroit. Indeed, the American inability to dispose of the problem of race may be the most basic failure of our Republic. The big cities have inherited the sins of our grandfathers and great-grandfathers.

Despite the emphasis on the distinctive black culture in recent years, however, I am convinced that we have more in common than we have to divide us. We have a generally common religious heritage, a need to bend the economic system to serve our needs, a desire for a share of the good life. Detroiters are mostly home owners, traditionalists in social values, believers, law abiding, concerned with building the good life for themselves and their families.

With all their basis for common interest, what divides Detroiters is race. Sometimes the words "city" and "suburb" are used to denote the two worlds, but the essence of the division is race, making people suspicious of each other, making them unable to unite for common goals.

In that fact lies Coleman Young's great opportunity. Here is a man schooled in the streets of black Detroit, but also schooled in the white-dominated world of state and national politics; a man who knows how to fight for principle in a world ruled by pragmatism.

I do not know what Coleman Young will do with this opportunity. I do not know whether the black voters who gave him his victory or the whites who fought against it will let him do what he ought. The new mayor may have trouble even getting a handle on the city's stubborn and often clumsy bureaucracy. Some unions may try to undermine him, others to exploit his ties to their movement.

Some people, in weariness or fear or disgust, may join the multitudes who have already given up on the city.

But what this city is celebrating this week is truly an opportunity. It has been a happy week.

If Coleman Young is a good leader, he has a chance such as no one else has ever had to bank the fires of racial hate, to make Detroit more a dream and less a nightmare.

The practical and tangible needs of the city are, of course, basic. If the new mayor can see that the garbage is picked up and the streets and parks are cleaned and the police are fair and efficient, that will be enough for many people. That in itself will be a challenge. Mayor Young has made no secret that he admires the ability of such mayors as Orville Hubbard and Richard Daley to see that such things get done.

The real test will be less physical than psychic. Detroit suffers more from a sickness of the spirit than from a terminal physical illness. If the new mayor can tend to the need for a cure for our world-weariness and our lack of confidence, the rest is more likely to come.

This week is a good beginning. The festivities have had flair and verve and an unaccustomed self-confidence.

It will, though, be a long four years, and the record will be made more on substance for the long pull than on style for the short run.

Let us have a dream, though; let us dream of a city of peace and a city of hope. And let us build our city — together.

A breakdown of U.S. economic dream

Ill fares the land, to hastening ills a prey,
Where wealth accumulates, and men decay;
Princes and lords may flourish, or may fade;
A breath can make them, as a breath has made;
But a bold peasantry, their country's pride,
When once destroyed, can never be supplied.

When I drive the streets of Detroit and see the faded, vandalized, boarded-up HUD houses, I feel a surge of concern not unlike that expressed by Goldsmith about the desolation of a village in the English countryside.

And if you couple the abandoned houses and the broken dreams they represent with some other things — the high cost of automobiles, the high cost of home ownership, the high cost of sending your child to college, the resegregation of much of the city, the decline in job opportunities — I see a real danger to "a bold peasantry, their country's pride."

Goldsmith was, of course, referring to English country life in the 18th Century and to a social class that has never existed in the United States.

But in the sense that there is a class of honest working people who have made up the backbone of American society and who are threatened, now, by changing economic and social conditions, the poem seems relevant to Detroit

Nov. 30, 1975

We face — in the question of whether economic opportunity can be open to most Americans — an issue on which our survival may turn.

and the United States today.

The redeeming virtue of American society since its beginnings has been a certain fluidity. Blacks were mostly excluded from it, to be sure.

But in the cities of the North and Northeast, there was at least some sense that there were few impenetrable class barriers. Some of it may have been an illusion; many people were in fact prisoners of their social class.

The great dream of the first two-thirds of the 20th Century in the United States, though, particularly in the post-World War II era, has been that every family could aspire to the trappings of middle-class status: home ownership, one or two cars, college as at least a possibility for the kids, consumer goods.

Mass production was to make goods available at a reasonable price that a mass audience could buy. Out of the concept of mass production for a mass consumer market has come the great American industrial complex.

And if the United States has always had its share of conflict and its radical movements, the edge was generally taken off the conflict by the idea that change was possible. There always was the possibility of more land, more opportunity, somewhere on this vast continent.

Somehow these last few years, we have begun to disrupt that process. Many people have begun to be priced out of the new housing market. Cars are less affordable. The energy and resource shortage means that there is less to divide up and hence more to fight over.

The reasons have been varied. Labor itself ran some costs up so that laboring folks themselves could no longer afford the products. The old liberal answers that kept the society intact in the '30s and '40s failed, or seemed to fail.

Seven years of Republican economic doctrine, perhaps misapplied, have tended to impose heavy sacrifices on the poor and the lower middle class. In some instances, monopolies and cartels have eliminated the free market as an effective check on prices. Federal deficits have helped to drive up the costs of obtaining money.

The results could well be the creation of a more stratified society than we have had before, and perhaps more than we can stand as a society.

Should this happen, it would be particularly unfortunate for America's blacks. They were in a caste system all along, especially in the South, and were left out of the fluid American society to a great extent.

Lyndon Johnson began to make some real changes in the status of blacks in the middle '60s. The creation of a black middle class — an essential element of a stable America — has been going on for years.

Not much of that happens, however, in a time of high unemployment, continuing inflation and declining real income.

It is probably pompous and pretentious to talk of anything as "the central issue of our time." Yet it seems to me we face — in the question of whether economic opportunity can be open to most Americans — an issue on which our survival may turn.

Nowhere in America is this issue more clearly joined than in Detroit, and nowhere is the outcome more in doubt. Detroit, where so many have come for so long seeking the better life. Detroit, where in so many neighborhoods, as in Goldsmith's village, "desolation saddens all thy green."

City's renaissance must extend to people

From the shining towers of the Renaissance Center, looking out over the city, one can see beyond the frustrations of today to the possibilities that exist.

Above all, of course, there is the river, with more of its beauty and its potential apparent from up there in one of the towers than you have been able to see before. The Detroit River is a beautiful stream, and while its recovery still has far to go, it is well on its way to being restored to health and life.

With the fall colors, you are reminded how many trees the city has, how much green space and open space are gradually being introduced, especially around the Civic Center area.

You see the freeway grid, a curse sometimes, but a great potential source of free movement. You understand doubly how essential it is to make those freeways as safe as they can possibly be made. Once again, a little Detroit chauvinism crops up in my thinking: Why can't this city and this state, of all cities and states, make the freeways safe from crime and, insofar as possible, from accident?

For the first time, you notice how big an area the Eastern Market expansion

OCT. 10, 1976

This city — this metropolitan area with its 4.5 million people — has too much potential, too much history, too much spirit and spunk and character among its people to succumb to the malaise and the pessimism.

embraces and how it will round out the market, cradling it in the elbow of the Chrysler and Fisher Freeways. You say a silent prayer that the improvement won't foul up the market. The crowding, the bustle, the cheek-to-jowl bazaar atmosphere are so essential.

Dear God, don't let us be undone by progress there. Remember what Al Taubman, the patron saint of shopping centers, says about sidewalks and people places: Keep 'em crowded. That sense of bustle and activity is important.

Eastern Market demonstrates that truth virtually every Saturday morning.

Something else you see from these shining towers is that there is beginning to be some ripple effect two or three streets back from the river north of Jefferson. You can see the construction, the reshaping of streets, the improvement in the appearance of things.

Beyond, of course, the effect is not stimulation, but decline. Up around Grand Circus Park, the buildings are still there, visible in the twilight. But you know that there are too many instances where the buildings are no longer filled, where the shops are struggling just to stay open, where what used to be grand old hotels are being turned into boarded-up hulks.

You know that, apart from the effects of crime and rumors of crime, no one has a really strong conception of how to turn the Grand Circus area around, how to give it life and purpose. You know that some such conception is, in its way, as much a key to downtown as the riverfront.

You hope that the occasional plans you hear about, which mostly seem to be made of gossamer, will take on substance.

Seeing the city from up in this tower, sensing its potential beauty and strength, you remember another recent evening, when you drove through darkened streets to see a friend in one of the Medical Center hospitals. The Medical Center has taken on even more shape since last you were there; it is better lighted, more open, something less like the dark side of the moon.

Still, the plague of fear has made us wary of shadows, distrustful of one another, tense about the possibility of crime. Is it an exaggerated fear? Probably. Does that mean the fear is any less substantive? No.

Looking at the city in these two ways — from the shining tower beside the river as well as from the dark and all too lonely streets at night — you know that we just have to win the war against crime and against fear.

This city — this metropolitan area with its 4.5 million people — has too much potential, too much history, too much spirit and spunk and character among its people to succumb to the malaise and the pessimism.

Detroit has a bad press, much of it worse than we deserve. I have occasionally lashed out at some of it. Detroit does need more intelligent and more effective public relations, so that this city's troubles are at least kept in the context of urban difficulties across the country.

But Detroit will never win out over its problems if it approaches this sense of malaise as a mere media problem. What I think we ought to do is to set out to show that even a burly, brawling, beer-drinking kind of town does not have to accept violence as a given of urban life.

The Free Press crime series recently pointed out some important directions. It focused attention on a whole list of ways in which we have let the system break down. It has already set in motion a number of steps to improve the situation. We have been too tolerant of the weaknesses of the system and the failures of the people who are supposed to make the system work.

I do not mean to say that the system of criminal justice can restore the safety and order of our streets. But it can be the start of the turnaround.

I believe deeply now that what we face in all of America, and especially in urban America, is the need to restore legitimate authority. A lot of corrosive forces through the '50s, '60s and early '70s eroded the sense of restraint and mutual forbearance that keeps most of us from hitting each other on the head, most of the time.

It is not going to be easy to restore that respect for legitimate authority. But we can no longer shrink from trying to do it — in an orderly way, with attention to due process, with respect for rights, but with firmness and strength. It will mean that we will have to fight off the extremists who say all you have to do is hang people in Kennedy Square. It will mean we will have to sift out the spurious claim of constitutional privilege from the one that is legitimate.

On a long-term basis, though, we cannot realize the great potential and the bright promise of the city unless we do that. We will never provide jobs, build racial cooperation, reconstruct the physical plant of the city, restore the sense of urbanity unless we do create, again, a sense of respect for each other and for the legitimate authority of the society.

To overcome its reputation and its history, Detroit has got to do better than merely address its public relations problems. It has got to establish as fact that it is a civilized place where civilized people live and work, together, in peace.

There's still hope for the old town

The week had left me in too mellow a mood, thinking how much I enjoy this beat-up old town, and so early Friday morning I drove down Grand River Avenue instead of the Jeffries, just to bring myself back to reality.

What had left me thinking about how much I enjoy about Detroit, oddly enough, was a week when we were interviewing candidates. Interviewing candidates!

Detroit, I found myself thinking, is really like a small town in a lot of ways. Despite the hucksters and the media, much of its politics remains personal. And surprisingly this year, much of the anger of the middle '60s seems to have drained away.

Aug. 21, 1977

Detroit is really like a small town in a lot of ways. Despite the hucksters and the media, much of its politics remains personal.

The candidates — particularly the candidates for City Council and for school board — always teach me something about the mood and the temper and the problems of the city. In an odd way, the mood this time seems less angry than the '60s, less pessimistic than four years ago, less racially charged (so far) than in the past.

I find myself collecting vignettes, sort of cameo shots of the city, through the people we've interviewed.

One of the more delightful interviews we have had was with Billy Rogell, the 72-year-old dean of the City Council. Billy, the old Tiger shortstop, has a lot of flaws as a public figure, not the least of which is that he is a hopeless male chauvinist.

But as we talked this time, first about the city and then briefly about the Tigers and baseball generally, I found myself grateful for a lot of things about Billy: a kind of blunt honesty, a disdain for cant and humbug, a kind of crude instinct for applying horse sense.

Billy has a scheme about Traffic Court that makes a lot of sense to me: Put it on the first two or three floors of the parking garage the city is planning on Randolph. With the money the city now pays the county for the use of the Old County Building, it could get the city a first-class facility and one it needs. This is an approach the administration should examine closely.

One stand Billy took years ago, and with which the Free Press argued at the time, makes him especially dear to my heart today. He opposed the present route of the Jeffries, arguing instead that it should go right down Grand River Avenue. If he had been listened to, we might have had far less destruction on the northwest side in the long run, and today we would have one less decaying strip.

The old shortstop says he has been to more Tiger games this year than he has attended for years, and he believes the team isn't all that far away from putting it back together. That intrigues me. Even though the Tigers have been frustrating again this year, they are beginning to be a team worth watching.

Jack Kelley, another councilman, didn't come in this past week, but back earlier. Sitting down with us, he talked in kind of a stream-of-consciousness way about himself and his city. Even with his drinking under control, Jack is a much-flawed councilman.

But I found myself intrigued as he talked about his perceptions and his alliances. He is not what you call your basic, organized thinker. I have a lot of doubts about what he is worth to the city. Still, even Jack can be interesting and teach you something.

Even with some attempt to screen out candidates I know aren't serious — some of them we have interviewed a good half-dozen times over the years without detecting why they always run — we wind up talking to a lot of people who are just along for the ride. Many times, though, I find that they have some bit of insight that tells me something about the city.

It is interesting, too, to see how many people have struggled to educate themselves and to make a contribution. There are a lot of cynics, sure, but there are a lot of folks who care about their town.

I don't mean to suggest that I never met a politician I didn't like. Some of them are so dumb, some so crude and banal, that it's hard to endure a 30- or 45-minute interview session. Sometimes you wonder how organized society survives at all.

This past week, though, I found myself fascinated and daring to hope that we may yet work out a lot of what is wrong with us and our town. Even my drive down Grand River from northwest Detroit didn't destroy that mood, though it reminded me what a mess a lot of the city is.

Many of our problems are susceptible to the use of will and wisdom to solve. The black middle class is growing and learning. The mood is calmer and more rational.

What we have begun to do to straighten out the court system of this city is one of the more hopeful things that has happened. Can we do it for the schools?

Can we bring those crime stats down by maybe 50 or 75 percent over several years? Can we soften racial hostilities? Can we build a basis for hope?

I know we have to try. A lot of suburbanites have thought over the years that the city's turmoil was beyond hope and the best they could do was insulate themselves from it. It was a futile hope, for the long run.

This year, to illustrate the point, the Southfield City Council race is like a replay of a Detroit election of 10 years or so ago. The same tensions, the same issues, the same mistakes in a lot of ways. The inner ring of suburbs is discovering city-limit lines aren't protective walls.

What the city, the metro area, has to do is to try to change things so they work — to make the courts efficient, to help the police stamp out crime without becoming repressive, to insist that there be good schools in Michigan for all children, to try to see that there are more jobs for all.

In a lot of contexts, such goals would seem to be mere platitudes, meaningless and empty. Here, they represent the life and/or death of the city and its suburbs. They are devilishly complicated in the doing.

Still, somehow we have to keep trying. This city is still people, human beings struggling to make something work and to make this tough old town a community.

Sometimes I almost think they're making it. Sometimes.

How teamwork can make the difference

Only an editorial writer would see in Alan Trammell and Sweet Lou Whitaker an allegory for the city.

Anyone else would see them only for what they are — truly one of the most exciting double-play combinations in the major leagues today.

And they are that. I had not seen them live until a week ago, when they were playing Chicago, and then again Monday night, when they took batting practice against the Kansas City Royals.

When they were on their hot streak in the early spring, I was getting ready to go, and then going, to Europe. Besides, one of my rules for survival in Detroit is no night baseball until after June 1. I violated it once, during Ron LeFlore's hitting streak a year or so ago, and nearly froze.

Then when I got back, the Tigers collapsed so badly that it seemed hardly worth the trouble: just another year of false hopes.

But the other day, with both the older children preparing to go off to college now, it occurred to us that we hadn't been to a ball game, and summer was slipping away fast. Too fast, like the years.

AUG. 16, 1978

I was not really prepared, despite the sports pages, for what Trammell and Whitaker have done to transform this team. Their range and consistency — what an absolute joy they are to see!

So we went, and then my son and I went again Monday night.

To tell you the truth, I was not really prepared, despite the sports pages, for what Trammell and Whitaker have done to transform this team. Their range and consistency, their ability to minimize a small mistake, the sense of timing between the two — what an absolute joy they are to see!

It is so utterly impossible to separate the two in terms of evaluating them and their contribution to the team.

Sweet Lou has become the crowd favorite. He is a fetching figure: a skinny little fellow, looking like an innocent out of a Bill Stern sports story, doing it all, even hitting with more authority than a skinny second baseman ought to have. And I never hear that chant of "Lou! Lou! Lou!" without remembering the story of how puzzled and hurt he was the first time the crowd did that, thinking they were booing him.

As I watched him ranging around second base, I remembered how many times last year that hot dog Tito Fuentes would make a bonehead play in the field that cost us the game. It would be interesting to calculate how many more games he cost with his glove than he won with his bat.

But then I watched Alan, though it was mostly a frustrating evening for him, with some strikeouts where he looked bad. After Tom Veryzer, he seems almost loquacious. During one of those many pauses while Kansas City tried to straighten out its pitching, he stood there, chattering away, with Mickey Stanley at the on-deck circle.

Conversation, I know, does not a shortstop make. But it is nice to have a shortstop with a little animation about him. And so, so loose.

The rest of the Tigers are infinitely improved. It is the reinforcement up the middle, though, that has made this team, if perhaps not a bona fide pennant contender just yet, at least an exciting team to watch. After those awful days of June, they just have not been giving much away.

It is Trammell and Whitaker, Whitaker and Trammell, who have made the big difference.

Oh yes, the allegory. Theirs is a neat story: the gold-dust twins, kids so young and so good — so together — that it amounts to a sports anthology cliche. You want to watch their careers, you want the town to love them together, you want them to be named co-rookies of the year.

You think of Dr. King, and the speech about black kids and white kids. You think of what this old town has been through.

"It's been a good summer," your son says. And you remember 1968 and your first year in this grim, torn-up town, and you remember taking him at the age of 8 to the ballpark with his Tiger hat, and you remember being there the night the Tigers won the pennant in 1968.

"It's the first time in a long time it's felt like 1968 at the ballpark," he says.

Behind you, behind home plate, there's a little kid with a Tiger hat too big for him and his father trying to help him grasp all the action. You look at the kid, and you feel a little sad and a little envious.

Most of all, though, you're just pleased for the kid and pleased for yourself and pleased for your own boy, now 18, and pleased for the town.

And, well, if you get a little fanciful watching those two kids at second and shortstop, what the dickens.

Isn't baseball mostly allegory anyhow?

Pain is real; can the church be saved?

What made me go to Immaculate Conception for Sunday mass I am not quite sure.

I am not Catholic, and I am not Polish, and we have supported the building of the new Cadillac plant as, on balance, a good thing for the city.

The gentle priest, the Rev. Joseph Karasiewicz, had come to my office to plead for help in obtaining at least delay and if possible reversal in the decision to close the Poletown church. But I had decided I wanted to go to the services before I had talked to him.

Maybe it was a part of my own experience that drew me to Immaculate Conception. For years, I struggled with others out on Detroit's northwest side over the future of my own church and my own neighborhood. I was chairman of a committee that merged two Methodist churches, and I wept, again with others, when we closed and sold my church and moved to the other church's buildings. People have deep feelings about churches and neighborhoods; I still bear psychic scars from that experience.

> **MAY 12, 1981**
>
> *A little of each of us dies every time one of our grandiose schemes for the salvation of the city requires that we surrender another little piece of what we have been, what we are.*

I also know that death or consolidation often does come to urban churches, whether by design or by atrophy. So no one can be sure that Immaculate Conception can truly be saved even if it can be saved. Sentiment and a sense of nostalgia are not enough to enable a church to survive.

One can know all that, though, and even support the Cadillac plant as a brutal necessity if we are ever to halt the inexorable decay of the city's industrial base, as I do, and still be troubled by the pain of this neighborhood, this church. The doctrine of eminent domain is stretched in this instance; the ability of ordinary people to have the sense of controlling their own lives is compromised by such a sweeping change in the city's landscape.

At the service, I found myself thinking, "What if this were my church, my neighborhood?" I would hurt, and it would heal no wounds for anyone to speak of the greater good, the need to preserve jobs and rebuild the city. It would not comfort me for someone to say the neighborhood was already near death before the process of building this plant ever started. It would not comfort me to be reminded that death is sometimes a part of renewal.

I knew all that when we closed the doors to my old church. I believed then, and I believe now, it was the right thing to do. Still, the tears came.

So on Sunday at Immaculate Conception, I found myself stirred by the sobbing of the Polish women near me. I found myself angered at the ravages of time and the impersonal forces of change in the city.

A little of each of us dies every time one of our grandiose schemes for the salvation of the city requires that we surrender another little piece of what we have been, what we are.

The issue at Immaculate Conception is not really history, though there is some of that. It was built in 1928, and its real significance is more cultural and ethnic than historic or architectural. It is beautiful, and it was especially so this Sunday, with Mother's Day flowers providing extra color and with the regular congregation swelled by those who came out of curiosity or sentiment or a sense of sorrow at the death of yet another piece of old Detroit. But there are many other places of more significance, with more of a base for survival, and we have torn them down with scarcely a murmur.

Now there is a last-minute effort to save the church. The church lies toward one corner of the Cadillac plant project, in what will apparently be a loading area or a parking lot. Could there be an enclave that would permit the church at least to survive as a reminder of what the neighborhood was? And if it were permitted to survive, would it be more than an empty symbol with the old neighborhood destroyed?

I don't know. I have placed some calls to the people involved, and I will be asking some questions. I don't want to be part of a media show. It would be cruel to raise hopes that could not be fulfilled.

The choices the politicians or the community leaders or the church hierarchy made weren't easy. I'm sure they have thought, as I have, that what had to be done had to be done.

But is there no room now for the healing gesture? Is there no magnanimous act that could take the curse off this process?

I really don't know. I only know that on Sunday I found my heart with those who wept and prayed at Immaculate Conception.

(NOTE: On July 14, 1981, tow trucks ripped the doors off the building and a number of parishioners who were keeping an illegal vigil inside the church were dragged away by police. The church was promptly demolished.)

A sidewalk perspective on a struggling city

At dusk Thursday, the little boats hugged the shore of the Detroit River.

Though the fisherfolk must often think themselves awash in that busy waterway, it was a tranquil moment. No wake then, not even much sound.

The last slanting rays of the afternoon sun were bouncing off the towers of the Renaissance Center. That moment yielded quickly to the onset of darkness, and the jeweled lights of the towers provided a sparkle of their own.

Along the concrete-buttressed seawall, other fishermen were manning their stations every 50 feet or so. Again, a tranquil scene at dusk.

Downriver a ways, the plaza was a peaceful contrast to the ethnic festival nights. The fountain was on, and it was almost pretty in the early evening shadows. A Coast Guard cutter, gleaming and white, was tied up nearby. A high school graduation was just ending at Ford Auditorium, and the shrieks of the graduates enlivened the Civic Center.

JUNE 7, 1981

The city hurts, and it struggles, and it makes mistakes. But it forgives and it demands forgiveness. Somehow, it lives.

Walking along the river and later along the nearby streets on such a glorious evening, we were struck by the difference in scale and perspective that a walk brings. The lawn of Blue Cross & Blue Shield's headquarters, remote and insular from the street, invites walkers to shed their shoes and walk barefoot in the dew. The trees planted downtown are big enough to matter this year.

The bars of Bricktown and Greektown, enlivened by the presence of the Michigan Opera Theatre Pub Crawl, spilled their crowds onto the streets. The hard edge of the city is always there. As someone expressed it to me the other day, "Sometimes the city seems like a toothless, ugly whore." But the shadows of a soft spring night make her seem more inviting.

This was the night of the day when the Michigan Legislature had been debating Detroit's finances. It is little short of amazing that the Legislature could act. The program demands sacrifices, imposes burdens, requires commitments. Even for those who support it, the program is not a source of much joy. It is a prescription for continued solvency, not for deliverance. But solvency must precede deliverance.

Meanwhile, the city continues to struggle over its economic future. How do you rebuild the crumbling economic base? The revitalization of an old city comes hard; even something like the Cadillac plant project in Poletown evokes a multitude of conflicting emotions and involves a long, anxious struggle. The tax package is necessary, but are we really going to change anything? Will the state be able to foster a better climate for industrial renewal?

On such a golden afternoon and evening, you have to believe that cities do not die, that the big cities' lurch from crisis to crisis is deceptive, that there are an innate strength and instinct for survival that don't yield to defeat or despair. The long, historic adjustments go on — two million people within Detroit's corporate limits in 1950, just under 1.2 million in 1980. As Felix Rohatyn, New York's Mr. Fix-It and now Detroit's adviser in its search for renewed solvency, told the Economic Club last week, we are dealing with powerful forces of change, and we need outside help to try to fashion our responses.

Like the little boats hugging the shore and grasping desperately for tranquility, we bob and churn in the murky waters of city life, seeking stability. The tranquility of an evening's walk here is not like the tranquility of a Grosse Pointe stroll. Bob, churn, improvise, struggle.

The beauty at dusk may be deceptive, but I think not. Cities are many things. They are budgets and payrolls and taxes and mayors and civic leaders and Legislatures. They are also people and trees and boats along the river and an instinct for survival and bejeweled towers and a place to put your line in the water along the river.

Cities live by the wit and will of their leaders and their people. They require for their survival the commitment of intelligence and perseverance we have seen in the Secrest committee. They also require the love and patience of those who find in their lights and shadows an enduring source of fascination.

Detroit has survived a lot, and it has died a little, too, at the hands of those who have used and abused it. The city hurts, and it struggles, and it makes mistakes. But it forgives and it demands forgiveness. Somehow, it lives.

Community is an elusive concept, different for different people. Detroit always seems to me to be a community in search of itself. Sometimes I know what the community is; sometimes I don't.

Watching the little boats at dusk, walking beside the river, I was pretty sure I knew a part of it. And I was a part of it, and I was glad.

Even battered cities can rise to the top

If you and your world were young enough then, you will always remember where you were last Tuesday night, the night the Tigers clinched the division title. Especially if you were there.

I found myself remembering that other time, the night 16 years ago last Monday, the night we grizzled veterans rehearse to you ad nauseam, the night the '68 Tigers became champions of the American League.

We sat — Kim and Scott and I — deep in the left-field stands. I didn't expect much that night. After all, Joe Sparma was pitching, and Joe was the fourth starter in a three-man rotation — a hard-luck pitcher with a habit of lurching from crisis to crisis. And when the Tigers' third baseman, Don Wert, came to bat with the chance to drive in the winning run, I joined the general murmur of despair sweeping through the stands. Don was not much with the bat.

SEPT. 23, 1984

For one beautiful moment frozen forever in memory, we and our town and our team will be forever young.

Scott was ever faithful. "He can do it, Dad," he said. "You'll see." He did, of course, and that became the Night They Won the Pennant. As the game ended, we stood at our seats and watched the sea of people flood onto the field. "Look at all those people," Kim said. "Look at all those beautiful people!" We held hands, the three of us, and made our way through the joyous crowd. It became, we read later, a rowdy night in Detroit, but they and I were oblivious to that. We hurried to our car and home. It was enough for one school night just to be there through the game.

It had been that kind of summer for us. We had come to a city torn by the worst urban riot in modern American history, had found a home, and had found a community searching for itself and occasionally finding it at Tiger Stadium. We loved it. I treasure the memory of that summer still. Though the way home was then out Grand River Avenue, itself scarred and pocked with memories of that riot, the city seemed to be less bleak and threatening that September night.

It was simpler then, of course. When the Tigers won that year, they won a championship. There was indisputably no one in the American League better than they. None of this East and West business. Just the Tigers and the Orioles and the also-rans. Just a championship season. I have always thought something was lost when the leagues went to divisional play the next year.

Yes, it was simpler then, and the season seemed a metaphor for the city. Like the Tigers, the city was coming back. The long newspaper strike was over, black and white began tentatively to reach out to each other, the city tried to shudder free of its fears and its long night of terror.

This year, again, the city has yearned for a favorable metaphor. The long night of the recession has been breaking up ever so slowly. The city's hopes have been battered again, by economic devastation, by crime, by political conflict, by the hard edge of racial division. Recession comes early to this region; this time, for many people, recovery has come grudgingly.

So many times as we labored through the long recession, I thought of the words of the song: "Been down so long, it looks like up to me." Not since the Great Depression has an American city been battered quite the way the Detroit area has these past four years. You would almost think a place would forget how to hope, with so many benedictions being said over its prospects.

Yet here we are in September 1984, hoping again. It has been, like '68, a magical season. It — the 1984 season — has been, in truth, a better year, a year of always leading the league. The '68 team came from behind a lot, living by its wits, surviving on clutch play and a handful of real heroes. This team has been marked championship all the way.

Looking at Detroit and the Tigers, you have to begin to believe again. If an orphan boy such as Tom Monaghan could make and sell enough pizzas to buy the Tigers and see them turned to winners; if Kirk Gibson could see the boos of '83 become the resonant cheers of '84; if Sparky Anderson could have the patience and the wisdom to mold such a winner, then maybe there were hope and promise after all. Maybe there is hope.

In reality, of course, This Championship Season will not diversify our economy, or heal our race relations, or bring crime under control. In reality, it may not even be very important that the Tigers have won.

But to us here, to the scattered alumni of the Detroit experience around the country, to those who find it impossible to forget how much they care about this beat-up old hussy of a town, it surely does help. We will hope, and we will remember.

For one beautiful moment frozen forever in memory, we and our town and our team will be forever young. And baseball as a metaphor for life will speak to this town and to us about hope that can last the darkest night.

History will ask the city 'why?'

Those who argue that everything is just hunky-dory in Detroit, if only the local media weren't so negative, should have been with me the other day when I received a delegation of young foreign journalists in my office.

They were in this country under the auspices of the World Press Institute, an outfit that arranges exchange programs. They came from all over — Chile, Western Europe, Korea, Pakistan, the Soviet Union were among the countries represented — and I suspect there was a considerable range of political opinion within the group.

They had just had their first taste of Detroit, going out to look at the site of the new Jefferson Avenue assembly plant, talking to the United Auto Workers. They were planning to see others — businesspeople, politicians, a variety of people.

Oct. 29, 1989

If history stopped with a snapshot of this moment in time, it would judge Detroit, and us, and perhaps America as a whole, harshly.

A tall young man from Europe opened the session. "We have seen Detroit for the first time this week, and I must say we are shocked," he said. They could not believe the abandoned buildings in a country that acknowledges it has a problem of homelessness. I found myself struggling — somewhat ineffectually — to explain how the city could look so bad, how things could get so far out of hand. I tried to explain what I could about the history of racism in this country and about how it is that a prosperous country could include a city that has seen the kind of decline that has occurred in Detroit.

I found myself trying desperately — so help me God, Mr. Mayor — to soften their dire impression of the city and to point out how we have tried to get control of the housing abandonment and homelessness problems and that there have even been attempts to take the two problems and create a solution. But there I sat, seeing the city through the eyes of strangers, thinking of all the visits I had made to strange cities, feeling shame and anger that this great city has been so drained of its once-mighty economic strength and of so much of its population. Someone in the group — not I — brought up Beirut.

And what it reminded me above all is that if we have to worry about whatever the voters might do in November and if we have to try to deal with the pragmatism of politics, we also have to worry about the judgment of history.

The judgment of history may not be the same as the judgment of these first-time visitors. I truly believe Detroit, even in its present diminished state, is an important and, ultimately, potentially hopeful part of the American story. I am even hopeful about race in America, in part because of some of the painful adjustments that we keep struggling to make here in metropolitan Detroit. The Detroit story, moreover, will have more chapters to be written after the election year of 1989. I cling to the hope that its historic affinity for the mythical Phoenix will mean it will rise again to a new era of glory and prosperity.

If history stopped with a snapshot of this moment in time, however, it would judge Detroit, and us, and perhaps America as a whole, harshly. It would not find our excuses about crime and crack and the flight of population and the abandoned houses very persuasive. It would ask us how we can call the American experiment a great success when crack thrives and babies die at Third-World rates and the schools fail and young black men feel no stake in the society. It would ask to know whether we tried to say the city could be something more.

Well, I believe in a dream. I believe that people can live together in mutual respect. I believe kids can grow up without having to live with fear of the gun-toting teenager down the block. I believe schools can teach and pastors can lead their flocks beside still waters, and I believe families can be blessed and strong and hopeful. I believe we can start defining community in an inclusive and not an exclusive way.

The tragedy is that the efforts of honest people to find the way to achieve such a dream are so often misunderstood, so often at odds with the efforts of other honest people. I must say that racism and violence and justice and hope baffle me now more than they did when I was 21.

What I do know is that we have to keep trying to raise our sights and demand more performance of ourselves and others. I cannot be complacent about the challenging question put to me by one of the young journalists.

As we were talking about the contradictions in a city where there is homelessness and an epidemic of housing abandonment, one of them asked, in the fervor of her youth:

"Why hasn't somebody done something?"

Why, indeed! Wherever you assign blame, wherever you look for ways to repair the damage done, as you look at all the wounds on the body politic, you have to ask that same question.

Why hasn't somebody done something?

History is going to insist on knowing.

City landmarks get too little respect

Detroit is not unique in the difficulties it has in building and maintaining the public spaces and buildings that give texture and vitality to the city.

And yet, as we watch the growing debate over the future of Tiger Stadium, the fate of Little Harry's, the city's deal with Comerica to raze Ford Auditorium and build a headquarters skyscraper, I find it hard not to feel sad that the city has had so little respect for what is old, so little sensitivity to the need for special public places. And when I look at the devastation that has been visited on Washington Blvd. over the 22 years I have been here, I feel a terrible sadness for the city that was and has so systematically been blotted out.

MAY 13, 1990

I continue to be amazed and appalled at a city that, in the name of "progress," has swept away so many old neighborhoods — whole small towns, really.

In some ways, it is especially sad that, after all black people suffered in the days when "urban renewal" meant "black removal," a black-led administration has been so willing to follow the same policies. A part of Detroit that was worth preserving did indeed die with the destruction of "Black Bottom." We all carry our own special memories and our own special pain.

I remember special scenes from over the years that are bound up in my sense of my own history here:

■ Of Washington Blvd. on a snowy winter night in the old days, with the graceful old street lamps giving a special charm to a walk to the bus stop.
■ Of dinners in the speakeasy atmosphere of Little Harry's restaurant, with a

charm that endured long after the caliber of the cuisine and the service had slipped.

■ Of my No. 2 daughter's first visit to Tiger Stadium, of a wonderful afternoon when she discovered hot dog vendors and souvenirs and I watched Nolan Ryan pitch a no-hitter, and of how it felt to sit enveloped in the deep green of the left-field seats that night in 1968 when the Tigers clinched the pennant.

■ Of how great the Civic Center looked during those golden summer evenings in 1980 when the Republican convention was meeting here and of how glad I felt that at least that space had the look and feel of urban life about it.

The obsession with tearing down and starting over has been a Detroit failing for a long time. The loss of Old City Hall occurred before I arrived, but seeing what the restoration of the Old County Building has wrought, I mourn for that lost opportunity. Kennedy Square has always been such an architectural monstrosity that it almost profaned the very term "square."

And just try visiting the splendid old churches in the old Polish neighborhoods without grieving for the lack of continuity and the loss of identity. It is not just that too many streets are unsafe; the other tragedy is that the old character of the city has been destroyed and, in too many instances, there has not been something new and wonderful in its place.

I continue to be amazed and appalled at a city that, in the name of "progress," has swept away so many old neighborhoods — whole small towns, really. That's what seems so appalling to me about the scale of the mayor's plan for City Airport. If the Poletown plant for General Motors and the Jefferson Avenue plant for Chrysler were at least debatable judgments about what the city's future ought to be, the City Airport project strikes me as simply incredible. Where is the payback? What is the rationale?

Cities that really work or that offer even partial rewards show some respect for the texture of the old as well as a passion for embracing the future. They protect vistas that offer you unexpected rewards, or give a sense of peace and continuity. They find ways to connect what they are becoming with what they once were. I think of parts of Boston, or New Orleans, or San Francisco, or Chicago.

The mayor clearly resents this kind of precious nonsense. He likes to put the shovel in the ground, to see the new city rising whole on the ashes of the old. I understand that much of Detroit has not lent itself to preservation. The city was thrown together in a hurry during a couple of boom periods.

But the utter disdain for so much of the architecture and the public places that gave the city character is a terrible mistake. And the preservationists, who struggle to hang on to a few vestiges of the city's history, are not mere meddling dilettantes.

They know that it does matter that there are two bleacher seats in deep center field at Tiger Stadium where my son and I sat through an All-Star game and found ourselves bracketed by two mighty home runs. Sentiment does matter; I still get a lump in my throat when I remember how happy the two of us were and how great that old stadium looked on that summer night long ago.

Dear me, why can't we be more respectful of the need for a sense of history and an ability to connect both with the past and with the future?

An early frost led to a special friendship

If St. Peter has any taste at all for collard greens and any love of flowers, then he surely laid out a very special welcome for Ossie Summerhill over the last few days.

She died in her sleep on Sept. 13 at the age of 86. Over recent months, she had lost her physical strength but not her spirit. She was my friend, a wonderfully whole and sane little old lady, full of spunk and devoid of guile.

My friendship with Ossie Summerhill began almost 15 years ago exactly. On Sept. 16, 1975, I had written a column about my older daughter, who rushed me out into the yard in my pajamas and robe to try to cover the flowers against an early September frost. The column was a bitter-sweet comment about the changing of the season, in which I asked:

SEPT. 23, 1990

It was always nice to know Ossie Summerhill was there, always loving the flowers, always believing in the curative powers of collard greens and friendship, always understanding that we have to keep focusing on our common humanity.

"What matters most? I never know for sure anymore.

"Sometimes, though, at midnight on a chilly night, I think maybe I know a little:

"A young girl who tries to create a little beauty, who knows the flowers' names and who rejoices at spring and weeps at frost. A moment shared between parent and child. A sense of the seasons. The last tomato and the first red leaf on the maple. The stillness of midnight, and the splendor of the stars."

In response to that column, Mrs. Summerhill wrote to me about how much she, too, had always loved the flowers, from her childhood days in Georgia to her later years in Detroit, about how touched she was by the account of my daughter's vain effort to hold back the frost, about how much of a connection she felt to me because of the column. She had in her letter a wonderfully expressive line about "our common humanity." I was moved by her letter and wrote back to her.

Over the years, we kept up our friendship, though for years only by correspondence. She saw something she liked or didn't like and wrote to tell me. She was having trouble getting her Free Press delivered and could I help? Her husband was having trouble getting his eyeglasses approved by Social Services and was there any way I could help her to get through the bureaucracy?

Along the way, her husband died. She continued to live, usually alone, in a little house in Detroit on the north side of Hamtramck. She kept up her church connection; she made the bus system work for her as long as she could; and she kept up her flowers and tended her vegetable garden. She hadn't accumulated a lot over her lifetime, but she was proud and as independent as she could be. I continued to hear from her every once in a while, by letter and by phone.

Three years ago, she wrote to me about her frustrations with a leaky roof and how she was having trouble sleeping because the squirrels were having a bowling party in her attic. I wrote with some passion about how tough it had to be for Ossie Summerhill to think of another Detroit winter coming on and a roof that leaked because she wasn't quite spry enough to get up there and get it fixed, and about how slow the public agencies were in helping an old lady to get her roof patched before winter.

People responded. A roofer from Fenton named Doug Spear called me and said he wanted to fix Mrs. Summerhill's roof for free. A number of readers sent money to help with that and other projects. They responded, as I had, to the heroic spirit of a wonderful little lady whose speech still was sprinkled with the imagery of her Southern childhood, and who managed to keep her dignity as she lived out her life in the city.

She called and wanted to know if I could come by and say hello. When I went out to see her that November day, just before Thanksgiving, she loaded me down with the last collard greens of the season. On another occasion she took the buses down to my office, just to make sure I had a mess of collard greens.

I felt a special kinship with Mrs. Summerhill, in part because she had so much poetry in her soul, in part because my own mother lives alone, far away, and struggles to be self-sufficient. Ossie Summerhill, though, became for me more than a symbol of "our shared humanity." She became a friend, and she gave me more than I was ever able to give to her.

There is so much that is daunting about life, and sometimes overwhelming, especially about life in the city. It was always nice to know Ossie Summerhill was there, always loving the flowers, always believing in the curative powers of collard greens and friendship, always understanding that we have to keep focusing on our common humanity.

I'll keep on trying to remember all that, Ossie Summerhill.

Detroit desperately needs a healing force

Over the last few months, trying to deal with the gritty reality of Detroit has been about as tough and corrosive as I can remember its being.

There are days when you read the morning paper, and you think there is almost no way to push or pull or help the city toward any more hopeful reality. In Friday's paper, I read the story of Mayor Coleman Young's angry denunciation of the federal government and of the media, and I wondered how in the world we ever get past his sense of victimization and the simultaneous sense of many others that the mayor is more victimizer than victim.

Then I read Susan Watson's column expressing the anger she feels about the tactics the federal agencies have used against the mayor, and I read Jim Fitzgerald's angry account of trying to deal with Bob Berg, the mayor's press secretary, and with the reality, as he sees it, of the city and of the mayor's stewardship over it. I reread the editorial I had written about the sudden — although ultimately not unexpected — revelation that former Deputy Police Chief Kenneth Weiner had been an informant for the FBI and the IRS during a period when he was allegedly continuing to steal money from the Police Department's secret service fund.

MARCH 11, 1991

It is a sad truth that Leipzig will be rebuilt before Detroit is, that the scars of Poland will be healed before the scars of Poletown have healed.

At a time when so much that has been frozen in the world — from Eastern Europe to the Baltic republics to Nicaragua to Chile to South Africa — is coming unstuck, at a time when so many opportunities for constructive change are opening up, this city is mired in irrelevance and division. It is a sad truth that Leipzig will be rebuilt before Detroit is, that the scars of Poland will be healed before the scars of Poletown have healed. It may even be truth that there will be a balm for Soweto's pain before there is real joy on the lower east side of Detroit.

The mayor sees himself and his city as victims — victims of racist media, victims of a vengeful and perhaps racist federal law enforcement establishment, victims of an economic system that disinvests in Detroit, victims of history. All those arguments are in part true. There could never be reparations enough to repay people of color for the victimization that slavery and discrimination have represented.

But what can we do? Where do we go from here? I do not know how little or how much Coleman Young is culpable for buying or selling Krugerrands, whether he or anyone other than Kenneth Weiner knowingly profited from the alleged looting of the police secret service fund. I do not know because the kinds of standards of accountability that normally protect the innocent and catch the guilty have been denied us in this instance. I don't know because the normal checks and balances — the powers of the City Council, for instance — have been neutered in Coleman Young's Detroit. I don't know because the federal agencies and the news media are left to ferret out bits and pieces of information and to try to make sense of them.

What I do know is that the city is in so many respects crumbling before our very eyes. At dusk the other evening, I walked from a reception at the beautifully restored Old County Building back to the Free Press by myself. I found myself running a gantlet of super-aggressive panhandlers, hurrying on my way, irritated at the absence of any meaningful police presence, looking at the empty space where the old Monroe Block buildings until recently stood, past the old Hudson's building, past the boarded-up wonders of the Kennedy Square block on Lafayette. I looked at all that once again, and I tried to kid myself that there was anything hopeful about it. And this is in the heart of downtown, supposedly the beneficiary of the tilt in the mayor's plan to rejuvenate the city.

I thought, then, of the more abstract questions: Even if Kenneth Weiner turns out to be the sole real thief in all this sordid police fund business, what does it say of the city? Where were the managers, where was the mayor, while Mr. Weiner, under the watchful eye of the FBI, allegedly continued to siphon off police funds for his personal schemes? Why was there a mayoral consulting firm anyhow, whether it dealt in Krugerrands or didn't? And what does all this — the utter mismanagement, under even the most benign of interpretations, of these desperately needed law enforcement funds — have to do with healing the city? How can anyone possibly feel good about the energy and effort that must now be expended to try to make some sense of the mayor's little $100-million mistake on the utilities tax?

When I came to Detroit nearly 22 years ago, I hoped I could be a healer. The city was divided then and polarized. I had this notion that the problems of the city could be overcome, that the polarization could be managed, that life did not have to be as corrosive and painful as it had often been for Detroiters. Over those years, I've watched the city struggle and, by my lights, I thought I was trying to make a difference. At some points I even dared to hope.

At this point, though, I must say I don't see a lot of healing going on. I don't see the emergence of a real partnership, of any real empowerment of people to solve their problems. I see everyone feeling victimized and not many people seeing how they can make a difference. I see a dream that has, for many people, very nearly become a nightmare.

And whatever the feds did or do, whether the mayor sold Krugerrands or not, I see a struggling city that needs a healer.

Seeing that, walking across the streets at dusk, I find it very hard to think of how in the world I can possibly do something that matters to heal its dreadful wounds.

Hope in Prague and Soweto, pain and division in Detroit. Surely there is some way we could assuage the pain here, too.

An arrogance of power disgraces the city

If bluff, bluster and charges of racism manage to obscure the enormity of the police scandal in Detroit, there is not much hope for getting this community onto a sound footing.

The trial of the former chief of police, William Hart, on charges of embezzling from the Police Department's so-called secret service fund is not over. The chief will get his chance to challenge the parade of government witnesses who have testified thus far.

Mr. Hart's guilt or innocence is what matters most to the law and the courts. What we have already seen, though, is an incredible indictment of the stewardship of Mayor Coleman Young and Chief Hart.

What is known beyond refutation now is that the mayor established and defended Police Department practices that permitted the looting of the public's money from this fund and the misuse of police power. The plea of police necessity was nothing more than a smoke screen to defend the indefensible.

MARCH 8, 1992

God help us, what a price the city has paid for this administration's insistence that it was not subject to the safeguards demanded of most mortals!

Even if you grant the validity of all the documentation the Police Department has been able to produce, it covers only a fraction of the money that passed through the fund. Far from jeopardizing witnesses, what has been produced thus far has only provided embarrassing evidence of how tattered the rule of law has become in Detroit.

I feel sorry for the many honest police officers who must be appalled, if not entirely surprised, at the accumulating evidence of how badly the system had broken down. Coleman Young won election in the first place in part because he was supposed to be dedicated to making the police accountable to the people. He and his Board of Police Commissioners have apparently been so long in power that they think they are the only people who count.

Where was the accountability for public funds? Where was the respect for law and due process that is supposed to protect the public from the thieves, and honest officials from both temptation and false suspicion?

What we have seen unfolding during the Hart trial should never have happened. The fund should have been audited and safeguarded and subjected to cross-checks. The Board of Police Commissioners should have focused on preventing corruption in the department, not on silencing an occasionally questioning press. The mayor should have had more difficulty in shucking off responsibility for the lack of effective policing of the police.

The guilt or innocence of Chief Hart is a legal question, and the only way it can be answered is in court. But accountability for maintaining the rule of law is a political issue and one we have to try to address even as this trial unfolds. Political accountability has been virtually destroyed in Detroit.

And so we stand in the midst of the banality of evil — of cash falling from the ceiling, of bills left on the nightstand of a mistress, of lottery tickets bought by the cluster, of open-ended spending for which there is no effective accounting.

Whatever happens in the Hart trial itself, this community is face to face with an intolerable and unacceptable level of corruption — the corruption of power in the hands of people who have lost the ability to distinguish between the public's money and their own, between the public's needs and their selfish concerns.

These have been bitter days in the city of Detroit. The mayor and his colleagues have done their damnedest to make the questions go away, not by answering them but by denouncing those who ask them.

But the questions accumulate, and the disgrace of what has been done to the Detroit Police Department and to the citizens it is supposed to serve grows deeper and sadder and more infuriating.

It is not racist to say this is an intolerable situation. It is not negativism to say that the Board of Police Commissioners did not do its job. It is not an ad hominem attack to say that Coleman Young had a responsibility that he failed to fulfill.

My Lord, what a sad result from an administration that began with such high hopes and reasonable prospects! God help us, what a price the city has paid for this administration's insistence that it was not subject to the safeguards demanded of most mortals!

Detroit has been disgraced before and has overcome the betrayal. Its history has been full of triumphs over disaster. It will overcome once again.

Make no mistake about it, though; what the arrogance of power has wrought in Detroit these days is a disaster and a disgrace.

City leaders turned trust into scandal

In all those years when Detroit's police secret service fund was going unpoliced and was being systematically looted, did even one of the keepers of the public trust ever remember that this was other people's money?

Did the chief of police, William Hart, ever remember that there are single mothers in Detroit who ride buses out to the suburbs and scrub floors all day and pay their taxes and rear their children the best they can, and whose contributions to the city's treasury are very hard to come by?

Did the mayor of Detroit, Coleman A. Young, remember — as he was resisting appropriate monitoring of the fund — that every penny in that account had come from the hard-earned pay of ordinary people, as well as from corporations struggling to maintain a decent balance sheet on operations within the city?

APRIL 5, 1992

Above all, we have to remember that it is right to be angry at those who, entrusted with much, have betrayed that trust.

Tell me who the Detroit-bashers are. Tell me again how the '80s were the decade of the Me Generation, and how the suffering of the people is because of the selfishness of those in power.

Tell me that there is no blame for our local leaders. Lay aside for the moment the question of whether the police chief was one of the principal looters of this cute little slush fund. The chief's trial will settle that question. But what we already know about the way the city failed to meet its responsibility in the use of these public funds is itself unforgivable.

The secret service fund scandal was no mere lapse in an otherwise exemplary record. It was a case in which the city administration, for whatever reason, short-circuited the processes by which public funds are normally monitored. In a city that needs every penny of police protection it can buy, the fund was looted of millions.

I believe deep in my soul that if this country doesn't help its cities, doesn't find ways to alleviate the inequality of this society, doesn't begin to make a down payment on a return to fairness, the good life that America affords many of us will eventually be threatened.

So I believe there is a role government ought to play in trying to assure that we balance our concern for the individual with a concern about community.

Plenty of people today argue that the very idea of using government as an instrument of social change is wrong — that it is statist and confiscatory of other people's money. They argue that government is inherently doomed to make things worse, that all we really need to do is liberate the individual, hope government almost goes away, and let the capitalists get on with creating wealth.

At some level, there's certainly truth to that argument. Governments do tend to become absorbed in their own needs, to be misused for purposes that are only tangentially related to the real needs of people or that, as in the abuse of the police fund, are simply illegitimate. There have to be limits.

I cling to the notion, though, that government can be used as a legitimate tool of social change, that governments can be run in a way that encourages the creation of wealth and fosters a concern for justice and fairness. I detest the view of those who think Detroit is a lost cause and that the very idea of social justice is a statist invention.

But what do you say to those who take the city's flagrant default on the police fund as confirmation that all help for Detroit is bound to be wasted? How do you answer those who say: Why try to help in the face of these outrages? How do you stand for reconciliation rather than polarization?

The only thing I know to do is to say, as clearly and plainly as you can, that power can corrupt those who would lead cities today as it has corrupted others in other times. You have to say that what has happened in Detroit has been wrong, wrong, wrong.

You have to keep examining your heart to be sure there is no taint of racism or anti-city bias, but you cannot be intimidated by the charge that that's what motivates you.

We cannot blink at the wrongs that have been done, and we cannot give up on the notion that there can yet be healing and new hope for the city. We have to try to listen to people who have worked hard and kept their noses clean, and who want only decent policing and good schools and hope for their children.

And above all, we have to remember that it is right to be angry at those who, entrusted with much, have betrayed that trust. People worked hard for those dollars that were plundered from the secret service fund.

Those honest folks asked only for an honest police department. What they got was an honest-to-goodness police scandal. There is, alas, a world of difference.

THE STATE

From Pigeon River to Lafayette Clinic

CHAPTER TWO

North woods provide a tranquil beauty

The north woods have a special therapy of their own, especially this time of year. They are a great resource, an asset to our spirit as well as a natural resource.

To arrive by night, during a snowfall, is to be transported, almost magically, to a gentler, less troublesome world. The harsh light of day gives way to the snow-lit solitude of the forest evening.

Even the thunder of the snowmobiles echoing along the forest trail merely accentuates the solitude and the tranquility of the night.

I don't suppose poems come unbidden to the mind of everyone who must spend a few minutes helping to transfer luggage from car to sled, but I found Robert Frost's phrase running through my head: "The woods are lovely, dark and deep ..."

Even the youngest child and the oldest dog strike out on foot through the velvet evening, walking the forest path to the cottage. By day, they are surprised at the distance; by night, the distances don't seem to matter.

DEC. 8, 1974

I understand now some of the beauty of a Michigan winter, which in the crowded city may be an impediment to free movement but out in the country becomes a way of life.

A son and I wait at the car for the return of the snowmobile and the sled. Not much is said. Not much needs to be. The night is cold, but it is beautiful.

To those for whom Michigan has always been the beginning and the end, the charms of the north woods winter are no surprise. But I am a Southern boy, and for me winter has always been only an inconvenience to be endured.

I will probably never ski, and even though I bought ice skates last winter, I may never master the splendid art of skating. I may never even fully understand the Spartan spirits who embellish their car bumpers with the "Think Snow" stickers.

But I do understand now some of the beauty of a Michigan winter, which in the crowded city may be an impediment to free movement but out in the country becomes a way of life. Maybe I can even understand the psychology of the hunter, who has a better excuse than most of us for wandering around the deep woods in the dead of winter.

The old dog who walks with us through the forest surely does. She ranges wide and chooses paths with an uncanny instinct apparently undiminished by her years of growing fat and sleek before the furnace grate.

Though at home she whines at the thought of venturing into the backyard to attend to essentials, here she moves out with enthusiasm along the trail.

On another night, the snow now stopped and the moon hanging low over the forest ridge, one can watch her move, a rediscovered grace about her gait, an unsuspected sense of adventure apparent in her manner.

If the still small voice of God can be heard, surely it is on such a night as this.

By day and by evening, the cottage by the lake, with its wall of glass to catch the sun, is like a pleasant cocoon. The open fire is itself a healing tonic.

Sitting there, with a good, simple book at hand, the city seems far away. Drowsiness comes, and comes again. The dog nuzzles the hand; the youngest child — for now the baby of two families, and the envy of us all — sets about to organize a game of bingo, and almost no one hurries.

The beginnings of ice on the lake drift back and forth, and the sun's light has a different aspect as its slow movements are measured on the surface of the water.

In early winter, one can see the cottages in the woods. By summer, no doubt, the feeling of solitude must be reinforced, as trails are hidden and cottages lost from view through the trees.

With the population growth leveling off, with energy more scarce and more costly, with somewhat more attention to ecology, one almost dares to hope that this sense of solitude can be preserved.

Yet even our best efforts sometimes seem to go awry. On this beautiful lake, a wide roadway has been cut through the forest for further development. The trees will never overarch this road; one could almost weep at the thought of the white birch trunks that must have come down before the bulldozer's sway.

Why should it be? A literal and maybe legalistic reading of the State Plat Act, I am told, or an overeager county board commission. In heaven's name, must so many of our efforts to use government for good ends come to grief?

Somehow, though, despite the occasional and maybe even common failings of the system, we have to protect and order and limit the development of these splendid north woods.

Even as we try, in the harsh industrial regions of southeast Michigan, to reha-bilitate and to restore, we must also protect and preserve. Much of Michigan has fallen prey to man's greed and insensitivity. Much remains, though. We need it; we need it the more while we struggle to restore the urban parts of our state.

And we need to love it, to use it gently, to keep the convenience of the snowmobile and the automobile from destroying the precious beauty.

It is a beautiful peninsula. Look around you.

The forest's value goes far beyond oil

Vanderbilt — Up and down the forest trails of the Pigeon River Country, the fruits of up to 50 years of forest management abound.

Here the stately red and white pines make a canopy, and almost a cathedral. There, the northern hardwoods give a glimpse of the Michigan that was, before the great logging cutover of the late 19th and early 20th Centuries.

At the edge of an aspen grove, there is a feeding range for game birds and the elk and deer.

On 90,000 acres here in north central lower Michigan, the state has re-created an almost unique treasure. It is not virgin forestland; there are wilder and perhaps more exotic forests in the state.

But here in a vast forest preserve accumulated under state ownership in a process that began in the early part of this century, Michigan has restored the variety, the beauty, the magnificence of

Aug. 31, 1975

How can you weigh the cost-benefit ratio of the elk or the hawks or the brown trout? How do you measure the value of solitude?

the land. The forest has reclaimed many a former farmyard. At the site of the old Grant School, the stoop, dated 1913, and the foundation tell of the brief effort to farm this country before the forest took it back.

This preserve has turned out to have a value scarcely even conceived of by the state leaders who put it together and the foresters who tended it with such care and love. For underneath a portion of this land — probably the southernmost one-fourth — lies perhaps $1.5 billion worth of oil. It could mean $200 million in royalties for the state.

Beginning in the late '60s, the state of Michigan — almost absentmindedly, it seems now — granted oil leases on most of this land. In the years since, northern Michigan has become the scene of what is, outside the Alaskan north slope, the most rewarding relatively new find in the United States in recent years. The trends and preliminary drillings and seismic soundings indicate strongly that oil is under the southern end of the Pigeon River Country State Forest in sufficient quantity that the oil companies are fairly panting after it.

The amount of oil under the Pigeon River Forest is maybe 10 percent of what has been found in northern Michigan, and with other finds outside the forest, the percentage of the whole is shrinking. Its value should not, however, be minimized; the oil there would translate into jobs and development, which many people desperately want these days.

The state Department of Natural Resources on Aug. 14 presented to its commission a plan that promised the best of both worlds to the state. It asserted that the state could permit expanded drilling and still preserve the forest for recreational, timber management and other purposes.

To many people in Michigan who had watched the DNR impose a long moratorium on the granting of drilling permits and who had followed the agency's legal fight to be able to deny permits, the new DNR plan was a shock. And even more shocking, the DNR's new director, Howard Tanner, came on as an advocate of drilling.

Trying to piece all of this together, I came up to the Pigeon River Country to try to see for myself. Was Tanner right? Was his DNR plan a good proposal for managing the extraction of oil and yet preserving the forest's other values? Can Michigan have it both ways?

The need to protect and preserve the Pigeon River Country is something I feel in my belly now. My two-day trip to the forest last week gave me some answers and reinforced my passion for the beauty of this state.

Tom Opre, the Free Press outdoors writer, and I canoed down the Pigeon River. We drove the back roads of the forest and hiked up to some of the scenic overlooks. We visited oil well sites along the southern edge of the forest. We tracked down a drilling rig on private land adjacent to the forest.

As the hours went by, my conviction grew. This is a treasure, and we have to protect it. Exactly how and to what extent, I cannot say with finality now.

I do not consider myself a hard-line preservationist and naturalist. I am not a regular camper, and I haven't hunted and fished much since I was a boy. I am not one of those who believe we can deny development at all times and at all costs.

This forest, though, is a major resource of the state of Michigan. It ought to be dealt with now, not on the basis of legalisms or expediency but as it has been for these many years — on the basis of the public interest.

How can you weigh the cost-benefit ratio of the elk or the hawks or the brown trout? How do you measure the value of solitude?

I know of no precise way in which we can weigh the relative values at stake here. In great degree the judgments are intuitive and subjective.

As I try to balance them in the scale of Michigan's interest, though, I know we must give them special weight.

Gov. William Milliken's actions this week give me hope that those precious intangible values will be weighed. I am pleased and grateful. After my two days in the forest, I consider it almost a personal kindness.

Intimacy, civility bless state politics

As our editorial board has worked its way through interviews with the major candidates this past week, in preparation for the Aug. 8 primary, I have been reminded of a quality about Michigan's state politics that I find redeeming and civilized.

Essentially, it is that the dialogue in Michigan state politics is surprisingly intimate and civil — a sort of discussion among friends who, despite their differences, like each other personally. It isn't that the atmosphere is clubby so much as it is small-townish. It is not uncommon to hear the governor speak of the speaker of the House as Bobby, or to hear Zolton Ferency tell, totally without malice so far as I can see, one of his famous stories about Michigan political figures (often, as it happens, Democratic figures).

I have often marveled at this intimacy. It has been particularly impressive these last six or eight years when we have had divided government in Lansing — the Legislature gradually coming under the domination of the Democrats, the Republican William Milliken in the executive office.

JULY 16, 1978

Whatever else you may say, particularly about Milliken and Williams, there isn't a mean bone in their bodies. They have brought a quality of civility to Michigan politics that is infectious.

In part, the pattern, which certainly was almost broken two years ago by the vicious U.S. Senate campaign between Marvin Esch and Donald Riegle, is attributable to the pattern set by two or three governors: Milliken; and in his own inimitable and sometimes rambunctious way, George Romney; and G.

Mennen Williams, now on the state Supreme Court, but from 1948 to 1960 the longest-tenured governor in Michigan's history.

Whatever else you may say, particularly about Milliken and Williams, there isn't a mean bone in their bodies. They have brought a quality of civility to Michigan politics that is infectious. Soapy Williams' ability to remember names and faces is legendary, but what is also true is that he conveys a sense of seeing people as individuals and liking them as people.

Zolton Ferency, though, tells a great story about that. Years ago, Gov. Williams gave Ferency his big chance in politics by appointing him as a member of the Liquor Control Commission. He did so without ever having personally met Ferency, though it was then, even more than now, an extraordinarily sensitive post, with a danger of graft always a hazard.

Several weeks later, Ferency was at a function where a distiller was introducing some new product that was to go on the market. Ferency was standing chatting with someone when, across the room, Gov. Williams entered and began making his way through the crowd, calling first names, remembering places and encounters. Ferency and the other fellow stood there admiring this performance.

The other fellow remarked something to the effect that Gov. Williams seemed to know everyone.

Not so, said Ferency. He doesn't know even the new member of the Liquor Control Commission.

The other fellow responded with suitable disdain. The governor would never make such a sensitive appointment without knowing his man intimately — at the very least, having a long interview with him and a State Police check.

As the governor made his way toward this little knot of people, the conversation intensified, and before Gov. Williams had reached them, Ferency made a $20 bet that the governor wouldn't know him.

Gov. Williams reached the group of people in the fullness of time and greeted the other fellow by name and recalled their last meeting.

As the governor turned to shake hands with his new Liquor Control Commission appointee, Ferency extended his hand in greeting and said, "How are you, governor? I'm Hiram Walker."

Without so much as a blink of the eye or a startled look, Gov. Williams responded, "Nice to meet you, Mr. Walker," and continued to work his way through the crowd. Ferency collected his $20, and a myth was tarnished.

The story aside, though, Soapy Williams did and does practice his political trade with a civility and a gusto that are awesome.

And Bill Milliken, now the second longest-tenured governor in Michigan's history, has had some of the same effect: He seems tirelessly and instinctively courteous.

Gov. Milliken chafes at the "Mr. Nice Guy" talk. He became as animated when we asked him about the question of style the other day as I have ever seen him. "I'm not going to change it because I can't," he said. And besides, he added, his style seems to have worked pretty well.

I have always been one of those who believe there is in Bill Milliken more toughness and purposefulness and persistence than he gets credit for having. But he is a gentleman and like Soapy Williams has managed to go through a long political life with a certain air of naivete and almost innocence about him.

Some time back, he was describing the kind of hard discussions that had gone on in the governor's office between Coleman Young, the mayor of Detroit, and Dan Murphy, the executive of Oakland County, over the issue of transportation. He was fascinated and amused. Coleman Young, in particular, had apparently really gotten into the discussion, in his usual roundhouse style.

"I haven't heard such language since I was in the Navy," the governor told me.

He probably had, but there is a quality of amused and bemused gentility about the governor that tends to elevate the tone of at least some of the political dialogue around him. And yet a Coleman Young, with his rough-and-tumble political rhetoric, seems to respect and accept the governor and his style.

I suspect this gentility and the general civility of Michigan politics may be severely tested this year. There are a lot of issues — abortion, parochaid, tax revolt, crime — that stir passions. There are a lot of competition and a lot of uncertainty about what, if anything, will make the voters latch on to a particular politician.

And, unfortunately, the result may be more heat and less civility, more passion and less communication. Maybe that should be. Maybe political dialogue shouldn't be excessively civilized, lest issues not be drawn.

Somehow, though, I hope we can remember, if and when this year's politics heats up, that there is something to be said for that better side of Michigan politics.

'Mr. Nice Guy' has led Michigan well

I first met Bill Milliken in the summer of 1968, right after I came to Michigan.

He was not governor then. George Romney was, though there are teenagers now who must think Bill Milliken the only governor Michigan has ever had.

Mr. Milliken was lieutenant governor then. He was one of a series of politicians I met that summer on a swing through Lansing: Gov. Romney, Emil Lockwood, Frank Kelley, Sander Levin, Robert Waldron.

My impressions of the group were (1) how civil Michigan politicians were and (2) how competent they seemed compared to many public officials in other states. They were serious people, trying to deal with serious business.

DEC. 27, 1981

Bill Milliken is a man of extraordinary goodwill, of quiet but strong personality, of considerable vision.

Bill Milliken seemed then the most gentlemanly, the nicest of a nice group of people. What I thought then, though — and what I think now — is something more: that this is a man of extraordinary goodwill, of quiet but strong personality, of considerable vision.

He is not — at least I have not thought he was — merely the Mr. Nice Guy that reporters have written so much about. I believe he has led the state in probably the only way it could have been led during this era.

When I came to Detroit and to Michigan, they seemed to me to be an amazingly polarized city and state: black vs. white, city vs. suburb, outstate vs. southeast Michigan. Bill Milliken has dealt with that.

He was an outstate governor who became the best friend Detroit has ever had in Lansing.

He was a Traverse City patrician who understood the importance of Coleman Young and the black majority in Detroit.

He was the Republican who worked well with Democrats.

He was a man of means who understood the role that working people play in this state.

He was a man who understood some of the pain and anger of women and the need to change the pattern of bias against them.

He was a lover of rural Michigan who came to identify with the struggle of the big city.

There were and are many other aspects of the governor's personality and character that can't be fitted into such lines: He can be and is frustratingly moderate. He has been exceedingly — and, occasionally, dangerously — tolerant of incompetence in others.

His, and the state's, difficulties over the chemical PBB reflect the effect of his laid-back style. He has made some mediocre appointments. He did not challenge us early and often enough to diversify our industrial base.

But I would argue that Bill Milliken's place in the history books doesn't rest on length of service alone but on some major achievements: Despite PBB, he has been a generally good conservationist governor. The bottle bill, the protections for lakes, streams, wetlands and shorelines, the efforts to deal with toxic wastes seem important to me in the long sweep of our history.

The role the state has played in the last five or six years in holding Detroit together has been crucial. It hasn't been turned around yet. But the governor and the Legislature have responded.

His sensitivity on race has helped us to deal with major difficulties and to moderate the anger that has marred so much of Michigan's history.

When I went up to Mackinac Island last summer to interview the governor, there was a revealing moment early in the morning, out on the porch of the governor's residence. The governor had just finished a 28-minute run. He was standing on the porch, looking at the Straits of Mackinac and the Mighty Mac bridge.

"There are times," he said, "when this office gets to you, but not up here. This house is one of the real fringe benefits of this job.

"Isn't this beautiful?" he said, sweeping his arm out across the panorama before us.

And then, in a playful comment that seemed both more mischievous and more competitive than the Bill Milliken image, he said, "Eat your heart out, Bill Fitzgerald" (one of his defeated challengers).

The episode was important only because it showed me, again, three things I believe about Bill Milliken: how much he loves the beauty of Michigan, how much he has loved his job, and how competitive a politician he has been.

I am frankly sorry to know that his era will be coming to an end. Whatever else he was or wasn't, is or isn't, Mr. Milliken is a person of rare civility, of decency, of integrity. He and his strong-willed wife are class people. We shall miss their influence in the state very much.

The Chrysler case: A rescue that worked

"Chrysler seems to be coming around nicely," I said to Gov. James Blanchard a few weeks ago.

The governor, who was the congressional champion of the Chrysler rescue effort, responded simply by symbolically wiping the sweat from his brow and breathing a huge sigh of relief.

It was a reaction that had mirrored my own. The Free Press had campaigned hard for the federally guaranteed loans that proved Chrysler's salvation and now, with Chrysler's recovery, stand to be repaid ahead of time.

The idea of that kind of federal intervention in the marketplace is always troublesome. I had come to support it for two reasons: (1) the massive disruption in an already disrupted Detroit economy that would have occurred if there had been a collapse of Chrysler Corp., and (2) a belief that Lee Iacocca, Chrysler's chairman, is one of the last of the real entrepreneurs in the automobile business.

I found myself frequently on the defensive about the loan guarantees. At a luncheon table conversation in connection with a meeting of the board of directors of Knight-Ridder Newspapers, the Free Press' parent company, I found myself almost alone in thinking Chrysler could truly recover.

At a dinner my wife and I had with Walter Mondale, the former vice president, about two years ago, he talked about the Carter administration's role in

APRIL 24, 1983

I find it reassuring that in an age of MBAs and computer whizzes and three-piece suits, the fate of a company can often turn on the force of a single personality.

the Chrysler rescue effort. He was proud of that, but he, too, asked the question: "Can Chrysler make it?" My wife said she was still very skeptical. I went through the reasons I thought it could — the restructuring of the debt, the support of the suppliers, the reduction of costs, the concessions by the workers, and, above all, the entrepreneurship of Lee Iacocca.

After I had gone through the litany, I thought to myself how hollow and unpersuasive it still sounded. So I added, out loud, "Well, it may be that they can only hope to get well enough to be a candidate for merger."

With the report this week of Chrysler's record first-quarter earnings, those of us who supported the loan guarantees and the other parts of the package are entitled to join Gov. Blanchard in his sigh of relief. It was a pragmatic decision that was easily caricatured from the Left ("welfare for big corporations") and from the Right ("weakening the discipline of the marketplace"). And it has worked.

It has preserved a greater degree of competition in the automobile industry than would otherwise have existed. It has held down the job loss in the industry. It saved the federal government a lot of potential costs that would have followed a bankruptcy. And it gave Mr. Iacocca the time to restructure his product line, rejigger his costs, and provide a new standard for personal salesmanship.

In Detroit these days, the business scene provides a good bit of evidence for the notion that history often is biography. Consider the impact of two men on the economic scene hereabouts: Lee Iacocca in a positive sense, William Agee (chairman of Bendix Corp.) in a negative sense. It is a fascinating contrast.

I find it reassuring that in an age of MBAs and computer whizzes and three-piece suits, the fate of a company can often turn on the force of a single personality. One person can, almost literally, make or break a company. It says that people matter even more than structure or management theory, sometimes even almost as much as the resources that are necessary to do a job.

Those who take the extreme free-market position — those who would never accept the validity of such an intervention — would argue that it is far, far better to let the marketplace decide who survives and who doesn't. Ford, they often argued to me, would have emerged healthier had Chrysler been permitted to collapse. Better two healthy American auto companies than one strong one and two or three relatively weak ones, they would say.

In general, the theory is correct. I hope the government, having seen the success of the Chrysler rescue, will not more readily intervene to save failing companies hereafter. It is an extraordinary action, to be taken only in extraordinary circumstances. Businesses do need the discipline of possible failure.

In this case, though, in this town, in this time, I am glad we were pragmatic rather than ideological. I am glad Lee Iacocca, with his monumental ego and his incredible drive, made it all work.

We shall not really know, of course, how well he has succeeded until we see, somewhere down the line, what his successors can do with this resurrected business entity. A company can be the lengthened shadow of one man for only so long. Then, it must have product and structure and research and money and staff.

So we won't know that for quite a while yet.

If Lee Iacocca hadn't taken a chance and been given the chance, though, we would never have had the chance to know.

I'm very glad this town and this country worked to keep the question open.

A ritual of ice in Michigan's north

In Traverse City one evening last spring, my wife and I stopped to see Bill and Helen Milliken. We were there to make a speech on our recent Russian trip, and it seemed a good time to see the former governor and first lady.

The Michigan north country is as familiar and comfortable to them as it is still strange and mysterious — after 17 years in Detroit — to me. Bill Milliken can turn lyrical talking about northern Michigan, and Helen Milliken's feeling about the forests and lakes is, if anything, even more compelling.

It happened that that weekend was one of the warmest yet in the spring, a set of golden days that offered the promise that the winter was finally being shaken off. As we looked out at Grand Traverse Bay, the governor described for me a phenomenon that I had not ever seen or known about, but that is apparently a rite of spring to those who know the bay.

I could see the ice beginning to break free from the shore here and there. Some-time soon, Gov. Milliken said, there

MARCH 10, 1985

There is a sense of unity, a sense of place, that is important and deep-rooted. It is bound up with the water and the land and the seasons and the people.

would come a moment when the wind would shift and the ice would begin to break loose with a loud noise from the shore. Then, within a few hours, the bay would be virtually ice-free.

As Gov. Milliken talked, there was such a sense of place, of the changing of the seasons, of the rituals that give life a continuity and predictability, that I envied him his northern Michigan roots. I have put down roots in Michigan, but it is never quite the same. I don't get back often to the farm in Arkansas where I grew up, but there is a sense of knowing the turf, of sensing the season, of understanding a place — even after all these years — that is important.

In a mobile world — less so now than in the '70s, but still a mobile world — we often lose that sense of place. One of the reasons a lot of Michiganians — there's my preference, plainly expressed — felt comfortable with Bill Milliken as governor was that he had somehow held on to it. He might have let the budget deficit get out of hand, and he might not have moved early enough on PBB, but he knew who he was and he knew who we were, and it surely felt right.

Other politicians might live and die by the airport, and they might lust for the Potomac, but Bill Milliken knew he was first, last and always a creature of Michigan, and more specifically of northern Michigan, and that was important. It still is.

Seeing the ice floes in the Detroit River the other day, I thought of that evening talking to the Millikens, of the beauty of Grand Traverse Bay and the spring ritual of the ice. I thought of a couple of very special summer evenings I can recall on a friend's sailboat on Lake St. Clair. I thought of smoked fish and the Leelanau Peninsula and chilly nights and cozy cottages.

I found myself remembering a sudden turn in a forest road, and the beauty of a stand of birches, and the chill of a ferry ride across to Mackinac Island.

These last few weeks, the roads being what they have often been, I have felt the need of some place warm, some place in the sun, and I'm going to indulge that need. This past week, though, I've begun to be able to look ahead, to sense the coming of the change of season, to find pleasure and beauty in the ice floes in the river and to revel in the sense of this place.

Detroit tends to obscure some of the reality of the earth and the lakes and the rivers and the sky. Despite the changes wrought by the Renaissance Center and other riverfront development effort, the city still often seems to turn its back on the river and to forget the earth — the place — underneath. You are more aware of where you are and what this state is elsewhere, out in the country.

A researcher from the East, working with us here at the Free Press, remarked last week that Michigan is a political entity rather than a physical reality. Someone long ago, she said, just put it on a map. It was one of the few misjudgments she made in a complex and impressive presentation.

Michigan is, of course, a lot of realities with a multitude of shadings. When it is as far to Ironwood as to New York, there's room for a lot of shadings. And the reality is, of course, like a kaleidoscope.

There is, though, a sense of unity, a sense of place, that is important and deep-rooted. It is bound up with the water and the land and the seasons and the people.

It reasserts itself in the breaking up of the winter ice.

It may be a little early yet on Grand Traverse Bay.

But it will come.

The Sun Belt states have nothing on us

Neither my adopted state, Michigan, nor my native state, Arkansas, has ever made much of their sisterhood, but in fact these two states were paired for admission to the Union under the Missouri Compromise.

Arkansas, admitted to the Union in 1836, will celebrate its sesquicentennial next year. Michigan, admitted in 1837, will observe its 150th birthday in 1987. The balance by which the Union was to be held together was kept: one slave state, one free.

Michigan went on to become, in 1854, the fertile ground on which the anti-slavery Republican Party had its beginnings. Arkansas went on to what I have always felt — despite the best efforts of chauvinistic history textbooks — was a desultory role in the tragic rebellion of the Southern states.

Michigan was the heart of the American industrial revolution. Arkansas was always — at least until industrialists began recently to look to the Sun Belt — an agrarian backwater. Those same chau-

AUG. 18, 1985

The vision that shaped Michigan, a combination of entrepreneurial genius and the foresight to build some great public institutions, was not and is not wrong.

vinistic history books always pointed, with a perverse pride, to the idea that Arkansas was the only state in the Union that had every important mineral within its borders. "Why, you could build a wall around Arkansas, and it could be self-sufficient," our social studies teachers told us. A cynical friend later pointed out that it was also one of the few states in the Union that had every variety of poisonous snake known on the North American continent. I'm not sure he was right, but it was a good line.

In 1960, the year after I got my master's degree from Tulane and went back to Arkansas, the census showed that, of the 75 counties that make up Arkansas, all but a bare handful had lost population. The newspapers were full of anguished discussions about how to change the state — to industrialize it — so that "our young people won't have to leave home to find good jobs." People went off to places such as Dee-troit to try to find work. My mother and father had three sons. All three eventually went to work for big-city newspapers: one in St. Louis, one in Philadelphia, and me in Detroit.

Then, in the 1980s, what seemed the pattern of life and the relationship between the states in the 1950s and '60s almost, but not totally, reversed themselves. Under the onslaught of the 1979-83 recession, the sons and daughters of Michigan people went south looking for work in sufficient numbers to be remarked. General Motors decided to put its Saturn plant not in Michigan, but in Tennessee. And you even found glowing editorials — though not in this newspaper — telling you how much better states such as Arkansas and Alabama and Mississippi have managed their affairs than Michigan has, and how, if Michigan just cleaned up its act, beat down unionism and respected the free market more, it might grow up to be an Alabama or Arkansas, or at least an Indiana.

Well, piffle. I don't know where I would seek opportunity if I were 21, and I certainly do think we here in Michigan have got to get our house in order, but there's a lot of romanticism about the Sun Belt and a lot of nonsense about what it has done right. There is particularly a lot of nonsense about how it is unmitigated respect for market forces that has pulled up the region by the bootstraps. In fact, in Arkansas and all but a few Southern states, the reason their 1980 census is different from their 1960 census is that there has been a deliberate policy, directed by the states, aimed at building up their industrial base. The politicians and civic leaders realized in the '50s that their have-not status could be turned to advantage and that air-conditioning had canceled out one of the region's long-term disadvantages.

So most of the Southern states set up commissions — it was the Arkansas Industrial Development Commission in my home state, and Winthrop Rockefeller was its chairman before he eventually became governor — that were empowered to recruit industries, arrange tax concessions, issue state bonds, and in general do anything reasonable and a lot of things unreasonable to attract business to the state. Some few states resisted joining the competition; North Carolina, I know, held out for a long time against granting tax concessions as a way to attract business.

Michigan and other Midwestern states came late and reluctantly to that kind of competition. Finally, though, it became difficult to hold out against the kind of package deals offered by the have-not states, and Michigan got into it, too. The winner of the Saturn competition, Tennessee, may be correct in saying it didn't give a bunch of special considerations to General Motors about Saturn, but Tennessee certainly has pursued a deliberate state policy aimed at shoring up its industrial base. It isn't all just trusting to the free market. The state did take a hand.

The point is this: These things ebb and flow. Or, as politicians like to say, what goes around comes around. Today's population loser can change the objective conditions that caused that population loss. State policy can be used to shape, for good or sometimes for ill, the future. Michigan has no reason to accept the funeral dirges that some commentators and some citizens love to sing about the state. It is a good state, with a lot to offer.

And while I love my native state — while there is a part of me that will always be rooted in the lowlands along the confluence of the Arkansas and the White and the Mississippi Rivers — I'm glad I'm here. The folks who formed the Republican Party under the oak at Jackson weren't wrong about the historic forces at work in this country. Henry Ford wasn't wrong about the notion that well-paid workers could become a market for mass-produced cars. Walter Reuther wasn't wrong in thinking workers had some claim on a just share of the profits of their labor. The vision that shaped Michigan, a combination of entrepreneurial genius and the foresight to build some great public institutions, was not and is not wrong.

As Ross Perot told a Michigan audience not long ago, what this state most needs these days is to "get its chin up off its chest." I agree. Our future isn't behind us. It's in the second 150 years.

Was the fight to save a forest in vain?

When word first reached us about the latest outrages against the Pigeon River Country State Forest, in the form of a pained letter from Doug Mummert, the stubborn guardian of the forest, I felt a terrible sense of sadness and anger.

There is in my office, you should know, a small, hand-carved figure of a pigeon, with a little plaque that credits the Free Press, Tom Opre and me with having fought to protect the Pigeon River Country State Forest from the oil drilling that has now done so much to damage it. The little figure is a forlorn memento of a lost fight.

I remember standing out in the open at the end of a day spent tramping around the forest, arguing with Jack Bails of the Department of Natural Resources about the risks of compromise on the drilling question. With Opre, I had gone to see for myself what was at stake, visiting the oil wells already then in place near the southern end of the forest. The pressure had been on for a long time to find every spare liter of oil and to suck it out of the ground. There once was an energy crisis, you know.

SEPT. 1, 1985

The great compromise by which the forest was to be protected has proved to be no protection at all, and the worst may be yet to come.

As I looked at the achievement that forest represents, with its 90,000 acres and more than half a century of careful husbandry, it seemed to me outrageous that the state would ever think of reversing the drilling ban it had imposed on the forest. That position was scorned by would-be developers.

The DNR and its then-director, Howard Tanner, decided that the choice was not between drilling and no-drilling, but between controlled drilling and the unbridled rape of the forest. Finally, even much of the environmental lobby — softened up, in fact, by the promise that the state's dollars from oil-drilling leases would become the basis for a land trust fund — bought the notion of compromise. We objected but bowed to the inevitable.

Now, the forest stands damaged and abused, its water supply tainted by brine from the wells, its splendid silence broken by the hateful noise of the drilling, the achievements of all those years of husbandry marred by what has happened. Oh, the shame of it! The great compromise by which the forest was to be protected has proved to be no protection at all, and the worst may be yet to come.

Like proponents of lost causes everywhere, I wish I had been more dogged, more persuasive, more effective in fighting for something I believed in and against something I believed was wrong. Sometimes the fights you lose, the crusades that get away, mark you more than the ones you win. I am not a fin-fur-and-feathers type like Tom Opre, nor am I a committed bird-watcher like my associate, Barbara Stanton. I just know that I went, saw the beauty of the forest, and sensed how deep and important the threat to it was. I was right, but I was not effective in keeping the threat from becoming reality.

There have been other such fights over the 17 years I have been at the Free Press and in the 12 I have served as editor. I tried mightily to help bring about, in the early years of the William Milliken administration, the reform of our system for financing schools. My sense was that we ought to move away from dependence on the local property tax, toward more equity among schoolchildren in the state. We tried twice in statewide referenda and failed. I still think it was right.

But when the state, after those losing efforts, adopted the Milliken-Bursley formula for distributing state aid as a painless answer to the cry for equity, I finally pretty much shut up. Local control of school financing was obviously more deeply rooted in Michigan than I had thought. Maybe Gov. Milliken was right about the capacity of the formula to equalize spending on education, I concluded. For a while, it seemed to be the case.

Today, though, the state is more dependent than ever on the local property tax, and the inequities among school districts have grown worse as local school systems have been thrown back on greater reliance on the property tax. With tax abatements and assessment fights, the equity of the property tax is even more open to question. Even with the equalization factor, even with the so-called circuit breaker to make the burden of the property tax lighter for low-income and elderly people, the system still seems to me to be deeply flawed.

The moment to make more fundamental change in the system, though, may well be gone for a generation, lost in the confusion over school desegregation and local control and the inertia that works against change by referendum.

In those two fights and some others I could name, I guess I have been stubborn and impractical. Sometimes it's impossible to swim effectively against the tide. I'd rather remember some of the fights in which I've been able to win, where things worked. It would be nice to be measured by the successes.

Somehow, though, the lost fights, the lost opportunities, are what I remember. I wish we had been able to protect the Pigeon River Country. I wish we had been able to reform the method of supporting schools in this state. I'm not at all sorry, given where we are on both issues today, that I tried.

Soapy gave Michigan much to celebrate

More than almost any other funeral service I have attended, the "service of thanksgiving" for G. Mennen Williams was a celebration.

Oh, to be sure, there were tears. The homily by his son, Gerhard M. Williams Jr., was especially touching. And "The Battle Hymn of the Republic" and "We Shall Overcome" made the hair stand up on the back of your neck. Gov. Williams was considered a friend by a wide range of people.

Still, it was not a mournful occasion at all. For one thing, the grief was softened by the sense of how complete, how active, how varied a life Mennen Williams lived.

FEB. 7, 1988

This service was a celebration, though, for reasons more complicated than the mere sense of symmetry that Gov. Williams' life had to it. It was a celebration of the legacy that he left to Michigan politics: a legacy of decency, of civility, of inclusiveness, of trying to work things out.

That is Soapy Williams' real legacy. He made it seem an honorable thing to try to serve the public.

It was, of course, a Democratic celebration. Gov. Williams was one of the two principal architects of the modern Democratic Party in Michigan. The other one, Neil Staebler, was there among the mourners, as were most of the major Democratic officeholders in the state. They were celebrating 40 years of an honorable, enduring, progressive tradition.

Govs. George Romney and William Milliken were there, too, and so were many of the other leaders of the Michigan Republican Party. It was much more than a Democratic celebration. The long tradition of moderate and progressive government, which Gov. Williams began, has persisted across party lines. Gov.

James Blanchard, in his eulogy to Gov. Williams, spoke of the progressive tradition. The mood of the crowd spoke of the essential decency and civility that are the hallmarks of that tradition.

There are a good many people in Michigan today who scorn that progressive bipartisan tradition. The recent Republican state convention was wracked by passions spent on the notion that, with a sharper edge and more disdain for compromise, politics might bring us closer to utopia. There are Democrats, too, who yearn for a more ideological approach to public issues.

I think those who chafe against the broad bipartisan consensus, though, are wrong. I think we owe a lot to those — the Williamses and Staeblers among the Democrats, the Romneys and Millikens among the Republicans — who did so much to shape the framework of our politics.

Of course there were sometimes issues not confronted, sometimes policy questions that got muddled or lost. There are people even now who, in the privacy of their own conversation, curl their lips around Gov. Williams' nickname like a curse: "Soapy." As popular and as important a figure as Gov. Williams has been, it isn't necessary or right to deify him.

What he was, though, was a man — a decent man whose instincts were to widen the circle rather than to narrow it, who had about himself a sense of mission and who stimulated others to think their politics had a mission, too. Over a lifetime of public service, that steady, persistent sense of mission led him to shape Michigan's public life and its institutions. I think he shaped them for the better.

Gov. Blanchard remembered being 10 years old, distributing Gov. Williams' flyers in Ferndale, seeing the governor call a square dance. I remember sitting with my father beside a floor-model radio in a farmhouse in Arkansas, listening as a 12-year-old to the fight over civil rights at the Democratic National Convention of 1948. Twenty years later, when I met Gov. Williams for the first time, I remembered to tell him how much I admired what he had tried to do about civil rights.

That's how it is with a life as full and rich and varied as Gov. Williams enjoyed. You can barely guess at the people whose lives you've touched. Touch them he did! That is his real legacy. He made it seem an honorable thing to try to serve the public. Michigan, where so many of the forces at work always seem so much larger than life and where the conflicts might easily have been harsher than they in fact are, is a far, far better place because he did.

What summers are supposed to be

She was winding up a summer job — not in Michigan this time, but in St. Louis — and she was trying to fill her dad in on what the experience was like.

Despite all last year might have done to prepare her for it, the summer in St. Louis had given her some new perspective.

"I've been used to Michigan summers," she said, "and I thought that's what summers were supposed to be." Even after the Great Heat Wave of 1988, she had not been quite ready for the heat and humidity that settle over St. Louis during the summertime.

Afterward, I found myself thinking about what she had said. "I thought that's what summers were supposed to be." There are times, to be sure, when — especially in the north country — you're tempted to paraphrase Mark Twain and say that "the coldest winter I ever spent was one summer in northern Michigan."

I recently spent a very uncomfortable couple of nights in an unheated cabin in a sleeping bag that kept not quite covering my shoulders. At 3 a.m., I was not exactly thinking of a paean to Michigan summers.

AUG. 27, 1989

From the Detroit River to Isle Royale, the sense that we are connected to this Earth is strong here. We have to try to nurture and protect and, where possible, restore this gift from nature.

On balance, though, there is something very special about summer in Michigan, something that we take for granted, something that others elsewhere do not always understand or appreciate.

On Thursday of last week, the staff of this newspaper said its farewells to the departing publisher, David Lawrence, at Tiger Stadium. It was a very special day in a special place. It managed to be fun and sentimental, without being maudlin or sad. The day was crisp and sunny, and there was the softest kind of breeze blowing through the old ballpark. It was an extraordinary day, one that I suspect Dave will think of a lot when it is 90 in the shade on a summer morning in Miami. It was one of those Michigan summer days that literally warrant the term "golden," a good day for good-byes and for new beginnings.

Maybe what makes our summers so special is that we have such sharply delineated seasons, that you know from the edge in the morning air that we are about to turn the corner into September as well as from the calendar. In the Arkansas farm country where I grew up, there wasn't quite that same sense of turning the corner on the first of September. Here, you have to respect and allow for the winter that is to come; here, you have to savor the last precious summer days.

Maybe the sense of the seasons has a lot to do, too, with the strong love of the outdoors we have here, with our sense of place, our sense of caring about what happens to the shoreline and the lakes and the Earth itself.

Oh, I know there's a contradiction here — that Michigan's people and corporations have often abused the pleasant peninsulas. Only a few places in the country — northern New Jersey, perhaps, or West Virginia or the portion of Louisiana along the lower Mississippi River — have been more relentlessly befouled than parts of Michigan. This state has struggled since the great cutover of the 19th Century, which destroyed so much of the original forests, with its own impulse to abuse and destroy.

Still, the awareness that this is a very special state, that its beauty is to be nurtured, persists even in the midst of degradation. From the Detroit River to Isle Royale, the sense that we are connected to this Earth is strong here. We have to try to nurture and protect and, where possible, restore this gift from nature.

A couple of summers ago, I flew in a light plane up to Marquette. It was a mildly stormy day. We flew relatively low across Lake Michigan and up over the Upper Peninsula. I was struck again with the vastness of the lakes and the intricacy of the shoreline. I wished I had the time and the sailing skills to poke into more of those odd corners than I can ever hope to see. There are not days or years enough; there are certainly not golden summer days enough to explore all there is to see. Looking at this state like that, though, I felt a special sense of proprietorship for the place.

And so I did anew when my daughter reminded me of what it has meant to her to spend her summers here.

"I thought that's what summers were supposed to be," she said.

So they are. So they are.

Some state cuts go far too deep

With the war going on in the Persian Gulf, it's a little difficult to focus on anything as mundane as, say, Gov. John Engler's attempt to restructure and to reduce the size of state government.

But the danger is that, long after the war is over, Michigan's people will wake up to discover very nearly irreversible changes that affect the quality of life in this state far more than the debate thus far would seem to suggest.

Gov. Engler is taking his election as a clear mandate for a significant reduction of the size of government, and in that appraisal I suspect he is right. He is also taking his election as a demand for property tax cuts and a new emphasis on education as Michigan's No. 1 priority, and that, too, I believe is a correct reading of the public mood. And I further suspect that conservatives are not the only ones who are disillusioned with welfare spending as an instrument of constructive change; clearly, much of what we have been doing has not been cost-effective, and some of it has been counterproductive.

JAN. 27, 1991

The governor's approach has to be debated, challenged, and in some important ways amended.

What troubles me, though, is that the governor's targets are, in at least some instances, misplaced. I hope the Democrats will not permit the choice to be simply between draconian across-the-board cuts and the particular targets the governor has chosen. I hope they will insist over the next few days on a re-examination of the options:

■ Do we really want to jettison support for the arts as a matter of state policy?

■ Are there not peculiarities about the Michigan economy that make the wholesale assault on the general assistance program less clearly justified than many conservatives seem to think?
■ Aren't the cuts in mental health going to do serious damage to institutions and programs that are not only defensible but absolutely essential?
■ Could not either greater use of the rainy day fund or a program of incentives for early retirement cut the cost of state government or the amount that has to be cut with less impact on the ability of the state to deliver needed services?
■ Despite the rhetoric of the administration about protecting children, are some of the cuts going to hurt justifiable and needed efforts to improve the state's sorry record on the health and welfare of children?

It is one thing to reshape state government and make it more cost-effective. I am glad to see the governor recognize that the property-tax/school-reform issues are real. I continue to believe former Gov. James Blanchard's failure to grapple effectively with those issues had a lot to do with his defeat in November.

But I can't accept the argument of those who are riding shotgun for the governor that what is at stake is simply the dismantling of the Michigan welfare state. People will, I believe, discover as we get deeper into looking at the trade-offs that tax cuts are not the only things that determine quality of life. The governor's approach has to be debated, challenged, and in some important ways amended.

The Democrats, particularly in the House, which they have controlled for years, have not had a lot of experience lately with the role of loyal opposition. They badly need to take hold of what George Bush calls "the vision thing." They need to lay out with increasing clarity what really deserves defending and what doesn't, how Michigan can get more bang for its buck in a whole range of areas. And then they need to fight like the very dickens to see that government is both humane and more efficient.

Michigan is at an important turn in the road. This state has had a commitment to trying to deal with human needs. Many of those needs do require state involvement. The state plainly has to try to meet the needs more efficiently and in ways that are more liberating for the people they're intended to help.

The governor has laid out a bold vision of what he thinks needs to be done. The rest of us who care about Michigan, too, have an obligation to try to help reshape that vision so that it takes account of what we think Michigan is and ought to be — and I don't accept the verdict that the only choices are between a welfare state and a state that ignores human needs.

With a little more intelligence, perseverance and, yes, vision, I think we can come out with results more attuned to the real needs of people.

Mental care changes deepen the pain

As Michigan slips deeper into August, and we realize again that summer is scarcely forever, it is expecting a lot to ask you to join me, once more, in thinking about mental illness and the state's approach to mental health programs.

Mental illness is scary to most people, and the debate about public policy is hard for people to get their minds and their arms around. Even in the Legislature, there are seldom large numbers of people who take the trouble to master the complex questions:

Which hospitals, if any, should close? What programs could or should the state privatize or localize? How much can we count on new miracle drugs to liberate people from long hospital stays? What can we do about the mentally ill homeless? How can we monitor the quality of care in the complex and decentralized system that has been evolving over the last few decades?

AUG. 9, 1992

Shouldn't the state be strengthening, rather than weakening, the ties between research and treatment?

The debate easily becomes a caricature of itself. The governor's chief of staff, Dan Pero, apparently went after me in a recent speech to the Community Mental Health Association. He suggested, according to the reports that have kept filtering back to me, that I was simply fronting for the UAW and the state employees whose jobs are threatened by hospital closings. I was also painted as an enemy of progress who doesn't understand the benefits of privatization.

I regret that some of the governor's people still think this is simply a turf war between potential winners and losers, and that if they persist, they will fashion a wonderful new system that will more efficiently allocate funds. They've also tried to argue that what the state Department of Mental Health is doing is merely a continuation of what has been done under the last several directors.

I think they're wrong, and so do many of those who have fought the lonely fight to see that the mentally ill are treated properly and that the system is not made worse.

Twice this summer, on Saturday mornings, I've gone to meetings of people who are alarmed and distressed at the direction of the mental health program — not just the hospital closings, but the bullheaded determination to listen to no one outside the charmed circle of the Grand Rapids mafia and the community mental health boards.

On one Saturday, I spoke to the Alliance for the Mentally Ill and on the next Saturday, briefly, to the Michigan Psychiatric Society. Both those groups and a number of others over the last six months have given me plaques that suggest they think I've been raising the right questions.

Those questions remain:

■ How few hospitals really are too few, and why has it made sense to attack such attractive and useful facilities as Coldwater and Lafayette Clinic?

■ Can the seriously mentally ill throughout Michigan really get the longtime care and support they need from the state system, which often winds up being the ultimate guarantor of care that many families cannot sustain with their own resources when they encounter long-term illness?

■ Why has the mental health director, James Haveman, so isolated himself and so tragically shattered the consensus about the evolution of the system through which the state tries to assure the proper treatment of mental illness?

■ Shouldn't the state be strengthening, rather than weakening, the ties between research and treatment? Yes, there has been a long debate about the focus of Lafayette Clinic, but I do not believe there is a defensible case for putting it out of business or restricting its mission.

■ With mental illness already such an obvious contributor to the miseries of the homeless, why exacerbate matters by pushing further with a misplaced faith that drugs and outpatient treatment are going to take care of all problems?

■ Why not take more seriously the clear differences in the problems of maintaining adequate services and adequate monitoring of services in metropolitan areas?

■ Is it ideology, or simply a matter of doing what is right, to resist the attempt to have the state walk away from its role as a provider of and ultimate guarantor of services that simply have to be available?

■ Even though the treatment of chronically and seriously mentally ill persons costs more money and sops up resources that could be spread among a much larger number of less seriously ill people, is the treatment of the seriously mentally ill not the state's most compelling obligation in this field?

This is heavy stuff, I know, for a summer Sunday morning. But there are a lot of hurting people out there, and I remain convinced that the state is mismanaging the mental health system and making worse a program that was never really adequate to the awesome challenge of dealing with some of our most vulnerable citizens.

THE NATION

From Vietnam to Reaganomics

CHAPTER THREE

Confessions of a reformed chicken hawk

Call this, if you will, the confession of a reformed chicken hawk.

The reference is taken from a comment by cartoonist Bill Mauldin, who, when asked early in the big war stage of Vietnam whether he was dove or hawk, said he supposed he was a hawk, all right — but a chicken hawk.

That seemed pretty appropriate at the time. My trouble was that I held on so long hoping that Lyndon Johnson would work out. He was a Southerner, as I was, and when he began saying "we shall overcome" in those accents of the Southwest, it raised the possibility that he could overcome the isolation of the South.

A lot of us needed hope then, just as a lot of us need hope now. We weren't witnessing the current mayhem on the campus, but sectionalism was strong, Southern governors were playing with matches, and the trauma of John F. Kennedy's death had left us a shaken nation.

So we — many of us — tried to rationalize the Vietnam adventure. The Cold War rhetoric was still ringing in our ears. Even Bobby Kennedy had done a lot of talking about counterinsurgency. And it was clear that any Democratic president with visions of acting on domestic problems would have to prove that he was also tougher on communism than anyone else around.

MAY 7, 1970

How can one seriously argue at this late date in history that there is any conceivable result that could come from our Vietnam intervention that will ever justify the cost in blood and treasure and in deferred solutions to our problems?

Eric Goldman and others have recorded how Lyndon Johnson looked at Vietnam in just that way, as a sort of nuisance that was intruding on his main mission. He, determined to prove his strength of purpose and character, decided he had to be tough.

In terms that seem ominously fresh during the Nixon administration, he didn't want to be the first American president to lose a war.

Okay, so let him employ a little realpolitik. The moral issue seemed obscure, because wars are always nasty and because it seemed the other side was tyrannical. Balance-of-power politics has sometimes done more than idealistic words to hold the furies of this world in check.

Besides, what would you expect the president to do? All those peaceniks seemed to have plenty of criticisms but very few answers. (This is, as the Free Press has often said editorially, "the tyranny of small decisions.") How many times did old Uncle Lyndon tell us he had no alternative? How many times did senators tell us, "Well, the president has more information than we have"?

Of course there were doubts, but one swallowed them. Maybe the generals did know something the rest of us didn't know.

Even now it is wrong to put all the blame for the division in the country on President Johnson or President Nixon. The latter-day nihilists whose easy answer is to overthrow the system are scarcely blameless.

But how can one seriously argue at this late date in history that there is any conceivable result that could come from our Vietnam intervention that will ever justify the cost in blood and treasure and in deferred solutions to our problems?

Looking out an early morning window, watching the shadows and the squirrels play in the grass, one feels more a sense of deep sorrow than a certainty about what Americans who love their country should be doing. As one listens to the early evening sounds of children playing outside the house, one wonders what we are giving them and what further erosion of the sense of community there will be before they become adults.

Thinking of them, the incredible horror of it comes home. Is there any decision more outrageous than for a public figure to send young men to war for even a debatable cause? President Nixon cited President Wilson as the great war leader. Did he also forget the lengths to which Wilson went to keep us out of war?

It is worth noting that on the day the Kent students were being killed, the investors of the nation were giving vent to their anxieties and confusion on Wall Street. Down 19.07. It may be worth remembering, too, that some of the young National Guardsmen at Kent fell down in shock at what they had done.

The kids call the police pigs, and the president calls the kids bums. They are both wrong, though there are bad cops and there are bad students.

What we are these days — all of us — is human flotsam and jetsam, tossed about on a sea that controls us rather than letting us control it.

Or, to mix metaphors and borrow from Matthew Arnold, "we are here as on a darkling plain ... where ignorant armies clash by night."

But wait — the nihilists are gaining on us. We can't wind up with that kind of despairing cynicism and resigned despair.

As we look at those kids — the young ones who don't really get involved now, and the older ones who don't want to go off to war, and those who can't understand why people are getting shot on Ohio campuses — we know we have to do better.

A nation has a lot of obligations. Some, like treaties, are written down. Others are not.

One of those unwritten ones says that a nation has an obligation to give its young people something to respect, even as it calls on them for respect. It says we have to worry about such issues as legality and morality and whether old men should lightly start wars that young men must fight.

Somehow we have to do better by our kids, and doing better means realizing the horror of war and the shame of ignoring the history of Asia while we kid ourselves with the simplistic lessons drawn from the history of Europe.

Somehow we have to give them more than promises about light at the end of the tunnel and the "one last push" that is going to wind up this thing.

I remember in the early 1960s a time when Secretary of Defense Robert McNamara was offering the assurance that the United States would do "whatever is required" to preserve the independence of South Vietnam from communist control.

Mr. J.N. Heiskell, who now, at 97, is still the editor of the Arkansas Gazette, responded in the wisdom of his years.

"Doesn't he know," Mr. Heiskell asked, "that 'whatever is required' could mean all-out war?"

Other, younger men would later say that it was an "open-ended" commitment, and they would wonder why they had not understood it to be so in the first place.

Enduring values survive Nixon's onslaught

McGehee, Ark. — As the Nixon presidency stumbled through its twilight hours this week, all of us had to look for strength and reassurance where we could find them.

I found mine in the town where I was born, where I grew up, and where, a few days ago, we had my father's funeral. There is a continuity to life in a small town that puts Richard Nixon in a little clearer perspective.

Mr. Nixon, by forfeiting his claim on public confidence, by lying and cheating, has plunged the nation into confusion and even despair. What is surprising and encouraging is that the country has been able to separate as well as it has the fate of Richard Nixon from the fate of the Republic.

In the post office of this town one day this week, I overheard an old man talking with one of the clerks. "If he goes out, can they put him in jail?" the old man wondered. After a muffled response from behind the counter, the old man said, with disgust, "Imagine the president lying like that."

More and more, though, there is a sense that the country can survive Nixon's disgrace and go on. There is a sense of permanence, of enduring values.

Aug. 9, 1974

The strength of the nation has been its people — people who believe in the law, people who believe in basic honesty, people who believe in the country and its fundamental values in a way that transcends any particular president.

I always find that sense of permanence here. The presidents come and go; the vicissitudes of life brush back and forth; the land and the people endure.

It is not that people in a small town are better or even much different from those in the city. The difference is we know them better and understand the sense of community better in the town where we were born.

The sense of continuity is especially strong in the family cemetery plot.

Here lie my grandparents buried during the dark war years of the third Roosevelt term; there lies a niece, dead in infancy during the Eisenhower years; there an uncle who left us during the Kennedy years. And now, we have buried my father, here in the last hours of the Nixon presidency.

Life and death go on. The president matters less here than in Washington and maybe even Detroit.

The strength of the nation has never really been in its professional politicians, though there are good professional politicians. Indeed, many of the professional politicians — the House Judiciary Committee members, for instance — have been serving us rather well these last few weeks.

The strength of the Republic has never been exclusively, or even primarily, the strength of its presidents, though we have had many presidents who have contributed to the welfare of the people.

The strength of the nation has been its people — people who believe in the law, people who believe in basic honesty, people who believe in the country and its fundamental values in a way that transcends any particular president. Richard Nixon's was the mistake of would-be tyrants everywhere. "L'etat, c'est moi," he convinced himself — I am the state.

But he was wrong, and so now his presidency has crumbled. It has collapsed because he abandoned basic principle.

The silliest notion is that Richard Nixon has been or could be done in by his enemies. The people wouldn't stand for that. They have no love for the president's traditional enemies. They have no thirst for blood. They have been troubled by the persistent rumors of the Watergate misdeeds; they were reluctant to believe that the president could be either as corrupt or as stupid as he appears to have been.

Now they have the president's own admission that he lied to them and to Congress, and that is enough for the people. They know now that he has to go.

Let us, then, be spared pious proclamations that he is doing it for the good of the country. He is going in disgrace, going because his country will no longer tolerate him, going because he has broken his trust.

The scandals that have brought this administration down were not minor flaws in an otherwise worthy regime. They are pervasive. Even cynical men sometimes do good deeds, and Richard Nixon has done a considerable amount of good. In the end, though, they are undone by their cynicism.

So now, the president is about to leave office, rebuked, disgraced, shamed. And now the country will pick up the pieces, rally round its new president and go on with its life. Gerald Ford and Congress will get the support and the cooperation to which their legitimacy entitles them.

They will, if they lay aside the cynicism of the politics of the '60s and '70s, get the help they need to govern and to lead.

Men die. Politicians let us down. Presidents fall.

But the values of a fundamentally lawful and civilized society endure.

There is comfort, great comfort, in that.

Despite all, this is a blessed country

On this Independence Day weekend, I find myself thinking back to the first question put to me on the oral exam all senior history majors had to endure at my college.

"It is sometimes said," my favorite professor began, "that this is a peculiarly blessed country, that it was somehow protected by God from the evils that beset other people. Do you agree, and if so, why? If not, why not?"

We began ranging then over all the byways of American history — touching on the growth of sectionalism, the introduction of slavery, the often harsh commercialism of the 19th Century, the unevenness of the economic system, the frequent failures of democracy. It was, I concluded, an exceedingly fortunate country in many respects, but we could scarcely consider ourselves God's chosen protectorate.

As we have moved through the years since that warm spring in 1957, the love I feel for my country has not lessened, but the awareness of its historic problems certainly has grown.

JULY 6, 1975

The basic variety and richness of this pluralistic society are as much a source of strength as a source of trouble.

The problem of race is deeper and more pervasive than I, an Arkansas farm boy, thought in 1957. The violent strains in the society are more persistent, more mindless. The cities, which I then only understood as intellectual abstractions, are less romantic and more in need of clear-eyed leadership. The business community is less self-assured and less intelligent about its own self-interest and the nation's than I had hoped.

The self-discipline that enables a society to be free seems more fragile, less ingrained than I had expected. Civility has less of a hold on people than I had thought.

The years since 1957 have been tumultuous ones: the civil rights struggle, the promise — and the death — of the Kennedy brothers and of Martin Luther King, the disillusionment of the Great Society, the Vietnam War, the corruption of the Nixon administration, the calamity of Watergate. They were not easy years. Many people have found their textbook faith in an America that never really was, shaken by all they have seen.

Partly, their faith was shaken because teachers inflicted on them a glossy, phony version of our history: of Founding Fathers larger than life, of heroes proved, of unblemished purity. Americans should have known it was too good to be true. Americans should have known the record was more mixed, more complicated.

Not long ago in Washington, I stopped by the National Archives. I found myself moved and touched by the sight of those basic, original documents. Looking at those documents — at the interlinings, the footnotes, the compromises — you begin to appreciate how lucky and how wise those men were to devise a republic that could last this long and do this well.

Seeing there the compromises forced on the Founding Fathers by the slaveholders among them, I was struck by how incredibly flawed they were, and yet how fortunate we are that even with their frailties, they succeeded in building a republic that could evolve into something more just, more compassionate, more nearly universal in its application of the old ideals.

Ours is, indeed, a troubled society. It does fall far short of its ideals. Its cities may be living up to the cliche of the '50s, that they are essentially ungovernable.

Yet I think we still have a great and good country, blessed either by the mercy of God or the accidents of history. I believe that the conscience that drove us to pursue the Watergate story to a climax is clear and strong, that the structures of our government do provide balance and remedy for a host of ills.

And I think that the basic variety and richness of this pluralistic society are as much a source of strength as a source of trouble. The nation is a polyglot, but that makes for a more interesting and — I think — a stronger society in the long run.

We are going to be working out the troubles of this society for a long time. Sometimes the change will be evolutionary, sometimes convulsive. Always, the society will change, and maybe always it will stay the same.

The country has too much vitality, too much strength, too much spunk and contentiousness not to adapt to changes in a multitude of ways.

And maybe, in the very variety of its people, it enjoys that peculiar blessing of God that I found so elusive in my oral exam question in 1957.

In the aftermath of the Vietnam War

Oh, the brave old Duke of York, / He had 10,000 men;
He marched them up to the top of the hill, / And he marched them down again.
— Old English Rhyme

The other evening, several of us fell into a discussion of the aftereffects of Vietnam and their implications for the United States. Some people believe that, like the brave old Duke of York, we have lost our credibility by marching to the top of the hill and down again without accomplishing our objective.

My own feeling is that, though it will take time for us to feel our way back to solid ground, Vietnam was an aberration, and its aftereffects may be less long lasting than we might think now.

FEB. 15, 1976

Vietnam seems to me to have cured our megalomania without paralyzing our will.

But my view was distinctly in the minority in this discussion. There is a profound sense of pessimism abroad in the country.

Only last week I had to fill out a long opinion survey for some university professors — a survey that I thought rested on the preconception that Vietnam has changed us so radically that we will never be quite the same again.

Obviously, too — lest I be laughed out of court before I say my piece — any great event has its effect. Events do introduce profound changes.

Again, though, others plainly see more dire results flowing directly from the commitment to and then the withdrawal from Vietnam than I do.

One man said he thought it would have the same effect the Boer War had on Britain. The British, he said, lost their will to fight, and so have we. The self-confidence that sustained us in World Wars I and II has been lost, he thought.

Someone else believed that it had undermined our credibility and had left the way open for the emboldened communists to go on the initiative.

Lyndon Johnson argued in his time that the withdrawal would have precisely such effects — that whatever the appropriateness of our original involvement, the fact of our leaving was bound to be profoundly unsettling in the world. A lot of us thought that caused us to compound our errors tragically and to deepen our dilemma. In the end, we wound up throwing good money after bad, and redeeming none of the sacrifice.

There is no doubt that we have been living with deeply unsettling events: The debacle in Vietnam, Watergate, the revelations about such institutions as the CIA and the FBI, the corruption of government and of a distressing number of American corporations, the shocking discovery that we do not have a perpetual leasehold on the world's means of generating energy.

The effect of all these developments combined is bound to be unnerving. And to change us.

But will they — and particularly will Vietnam and its aftereffects — necessarily turn us into a crippled giant? Is the sun setting for the United States?

This year is a time of uncertainty. An unelected president is lurching along, with a secretary of state who may well have overstayed his time but can't possibly leave now, a Congress in which every other member is running for president, and a foreign policy now badly in need of revamping. There may be some American consensus, but early in this election year it is not clear what it is.

But I am not at all sure that the results are so dire, or our prospects so dark.

In fact, Vietnam seems to me to have cured our megalomania without paralyzing our will. The lessons of Vietnam are not especially welcome to a lot of people who still believe we should apply our power to every untidy situation in the world, but selectively applied, those lessons need not make us powerless.

In fact, the energy crisis has ushered in a sense that we live in a finite world with limited resources and need for responsible usage.

In fact, some of our institutions had failed us and were badly in need of accountability. I don't believe we should keep the CIA on the rack much longer, but I do believe institutions have to account to a democratic people.

In fact, the society has been accepting discipline with an acquiescence that frankly amazes me — accepting the sacrifice of jobs to bring the rampant inflation of the 1973-74 period under control, for instance; tolerating a radical adjustment in the cost of energy; improving productivity and competitiveness.

In short, I don't believe the uncertainties of this year, before this presidential election, mean that the Republic is doomed to decline. I do wish at times such as this that we had the flexibility of a parliamentary system and could call our elections quickly.

What we need, in my judgment, is not the restoration of our nerve, which I don't believe we've lost. What we need is the restoration of some sort of consensus, about foreign policy as about domestic policy.

The consensus is forming, but at a time when the politicians aren't sure how to read it; they run around in circles and draw all sorts of conclusions.

It may look like the end of the age, but in fact it is just a great democracy deciding where we go from here. It may be disorderly, but it isn't doom.

Humphrey: The human qualities count

Hubert Humphrey's campaign bus, as Theodore White described the scene in "The Making of the President 1960," was rumbling through the night during the 1960 Wisconsin presidential primary.

It was a cold night and a long bus ride, one of those nights when the candidate must have asked himself why he and John Kennedy were slogging through the lonely primary campaign.

One of the reporters broke out what White called "a bottle of fine expense-account whiskey" to help ward off the chill of the night. As the bus ride continued, Humphrey grew philosophical.

As they passed by shopping centers, he took his cue and began to talk about the growth of the chain stores and how they were submerging the little merchants. His identification with the little merchants — and the little farmers and the average citizen — was almost total. White wrote afterward of "that romantic, almost quaint faith in ordinary people."

MAY 2, 1976

In a political world that seems to demand and often produce plastic men, Hubert Humphrey was and is a marvelous human being.

Humphrey lost the primary wars that year, lost them to the Kennedy money and charm and to his own irrepressible disorderliness as a candidate. He saw himself, as White described it, like a "corner grocer running against a chain store."

The trouble with Hubert Humphrey as a candidate, then and later, was that his campaign lacked a sense of restraint and proportion. It also lacked that sense of fierce dedication that so characterized the Kennedy campaign.

As White describes it, Humphrey would dictate to a group of newsmen a stinging statement attacking Kennedy, and then take the edge off it by saying, off-the-record, "I'll have a lot more to say later, and it'll all be petty and cheap, too."

Hubert Humphrey was the happy warrior, exuberant, self-mocking, not a good hater.

In 1960, the interloper Kennedy defeated him in the primaries. In 1968, after he had put in his time as vice president, the interlopers in his party challenged him again, and though he won the nomination, he couldn't win the presidency. In 1972, he was the spoiler, embarrassing George McGovern in California but not stopping him.

So now, in 1976, he has chosen not to fight the interloper's fight. The Georgia Snopeses have already moved into the Democratic Party's big house on the hill, at least so far as Hubert Humphrey is concerned. And this time he, Hubert Humphrey, at least had the grace to realize that time had passed his presidential aspirations by.

What remain for him are the Senate, the party, the family, the role of counselor to and friend of presidents. As he said Thursday, "a good life." He will not be president.

Hubert Humphrey was and is a flawed man. His natural exuberance is bridled now, but it is there. His lack of a sense of proportion still gets in his way. Maybe it is just as well that he will never be president. There is enough on the record to make you wonder.

Still, in a political world that seems to demand and often produce plastic men, Hubert Humphrey was and is a marvelous human being. He was one of the last, best exponents of the progressivism and populism that once so thoroughly characterized the politics of the upper Midwest. He was a liberal who cared about people as well as humanity.

The older I get and the more I observe politics, the more it matters to me whether a political leader is that kind of human being, whether he cares about people. I have come to appreciate Barry Goldwater's human qualities, for instance, in a way that I never could Nixon's. There is a kind of craggy honesty and humanity about Barry Goldwater that has come through more and more strongly.

Watching a Hubert Humphrey or a Barry Goldwater age, with considerably more grace than you might have expected, I tend to care less about their ideology than I used to and more about their humanity.

A friend of mine used to say that the real test of a person was whether you could sit up all night in a bus station with him and still be able to stand him. Hubert Humphrey might talk your arm off, but I think he probably qualifies.

After Sen. Humphrey appeared a few weeks ago before the American Society of Newspaper Editors, thinking at that point that he might yet get his party's call, I remarked to friends that I thought he seemed like nothing so much as "an aging schoolmaster," lecturing, scolding, cajoling, teaching.

As he said Thursday that he was not going to seek the presidency, Sen. Humphrey expressed the hope that Jimmy Carter could be made to discuss issues a little more. And he added, "I'm going to help educate him."

Knowing a little of Hubert Humphrey, I believe he will.

Despite the factors that have kept Hubert Humphrey from being president, Mr. Carter could do a great deal worse for a schoolmaster.

Poignant memories of the suffering nisei

At first glance, the memorial to the nisei war dead seems totally incongruous with the Arkansas countryside.

It is cotton country, a few miles from the farm where I grew up, and while there are a few Chinese in some of the neighboring towns, there is not a Japanese American to be found there today.

But there, beside Highway 1, stands the memorial, erected in loving memory of those brave Japanese Americans who gave their lives in the European theater.

It stands there because, during most of World War II, that was the site of one of the infamous "Japanese relocation centers," to which the Japanese Americans of California were forcibly removed during World War II.

During the war, my father worked as a farm supervisor for the center. During the Depression, he had worked for the Agricultural Adjustment Administration and the Farm Security Administration; when the center opened, he applied for work there.

MAY 23, 1976

Now, all that remains is the war memorial, there beside the road, honoring the dead, speaking of the stubborn patriotism of the nisei, shaming the country for what it did to them.

By order of the U.S. government, and by sanction of the U.S. Supreme Court, the nisei were removed first to Utah and later — for 25,000 of them, as I remember — to that center at Rohwer, Ark., which was hacked out of the swampy bottoms of the Arkansas River country.

Most of the nisei had lived for generations as fully integrated American citizens. I have seen poignant accounts by youngsters who were thrust by the forced removal to live for the first time among people of a similar ethnic background.

It was ironic to see how these strange people — these people who looked just like the enemy — were more sophisticated, more cultivated in many ways than we who lived around them. The first paintings and wood carvings I remember seeing were those left scattered around houses in southeast Arkansas as a result of the time the nisei spent there.

The writings I have seen from the students tell something of the impact of the place on the new arrivals: The unceasing rain, the mud, the common eating quarters imposed on people for whom the family unit was especially strong, the Anglo teachers, the suspicions bred by war.

The yearbooks from the school are very guarded and careful. After all, it was wartime, and these people were living behind barbed wire. They were suspect. One notices in the artwork, however, a recurring theme: the watchtowers overlooking the flat drabness of the tar-paper city. The message was clear; the students were prisoners in their own land.

After the war, the camp was dismantled. The buildings were cut into sections and hauled around the countryside and sold. The first gravel on the road in front of the house where I grew up was bought by the county from the federal government, dug up off the roads of the relocation center.

I was a child, and I saw through a glass darkly, but in the years since I have come to understand what a travesty those camps were — how hateful it was that, in the panic of those first anxious times after Pearl Harbor, the country herded these people onto trains and dumped them into a tar-papered, hot, rainy place where they were something less than the full American citizens they were supposed to be.

Now, all that remains is the war memorial, there beside the road, honoring the dead, speaking of the stubborn patriotism of the nisei, shaming the country for what it did to them.

For years after World War II, the little memorial fell into disrepair. There was no one to honor the memory, no one to keep faith with the dead.

Finally, a few people with a sense of history and a sense of justice — my mother among them, I'm proud to say — decided it just wasn't right. Those who gave so much after their people had suffered so much should not go unhonored. Someone should at least tend the memorial to the dead.

So now the grass is cut, and some flowers are planted. A few veterans' groups have enlisted in the cause and supply some of the work.

It isn't much, but it's something.

Now, those years, that camp, those people seem almost unreal. Could we have done that? Why were gentler alternatives not weighed? How could even a civil libertarian such as Earl Warren, then attorney general of California, join the madness? How could Hugo Black, on the Supreme Court, give it sanction?

Those were fearsome years, and we should probably not stand too much in judgment of those who tried to cope with the grim realities of that time. Still, it hurts to think of what was done.

When I go back and stop by the memorial, I know how far we have come, and how far we have to go, on the long road to becoming a civilized country.

The blessing of being part of America

The trouble with asking an editor to say something fitting for a bicentennial day is that it encourages him to be even more pompous than usual.

Surely by now, every glowing tribute, every swelling phrase, every red, white and blue sentiment has been trotted before the dazzled eyes of the weary world. One more such pronouncement and we shall all be undone.

Rather than try to rise to the occasion, I would prefer simply to try to talk, as quietly and plainly as I can, about some of what the country means to me and of what I hope it can become. No immortal quotations, no epigrammatic tributes, just why I'm glad to be around for this 200th birthday celebration and what I hope it will call forth in the American spirit.

I am glad to be an American.

It is true — and we ought not to forget it while we are wallowing in self-adulation this week — that we have no monopoly on either virtue or the blessings of history or God.

> **JULY 4, 1976**
>
> *The line I have always liked best in "America the Beautiful" is the one about "mend thine every flaw."*

The British, for instance, may have more self-restraint than we do. The Swedes may have more of a sense of social justice. The Germans may even have a greater commitment to productivity. The Japanese may have more civility. I am not a chauvinist, and I see no more reason on this bicentennial day to lay claim to all virtue for our society than I do on any other day.

But this oldest and most stable of republics does have some strengths that, if not unique, are at least important to those of us who are Americans.

The first, of course, is the land itself. Though much is taken, much abides, as Tennyson said in another context. Ours is a broad and beautiful continent, still with a lot of room to breathe. The countryside has a stubborn way of defying our best efforts to defile it. And in recent years, we seem to be discovering a new sense of appreciation and respect for the land. The Detroit River, for instance, and Lake Erie are demonstrably cleaner, though much remains to be done. In the air, on and in the waters, and on the land itself, there is some commitment to letting the land be itself — beautiful, varied, full of resources, supportive of the good life.

Equally as important as the land to me are the pluralism, the variety, the complexity of the people. I grew up in a small Southern town and did not fully comprehend the variety of the population until I was grown.

The best evidence from the history of the human race is that such a country cannot endure. Race does tend to divide. Religious differences do tend to drive people to misunderstand one another. People do tend to justify their own kind and to belittle or detract from those who are unlike them.

Yet despite all the evidence in the world that people can't live in peace with their differences, I think we're making headway. The curse of race has not been conquered, not by any means, but I think the last quarter century has brought us face to face with our failings and our opportunities.

The variety is troublesome. It may eventually undo us, though I think not. I like to believe, I do believe, that men of goodwill are going to work out the problems and make of the United States a country where we take pleasure in our diversity and yet feel strongly the bond of our common humanity.

I am grateful, too, for the base of our economic strength. It was not our peculiar genius, necessarily, that made it. It was this vast and rich continent, the existence of a unified and in some ways protected marketplace, the presence of people who owe their education to some other country but who have found this a hospitable place to work and build and make money.

I am glad that we have been able, so far, to respond to social needs within the framework of a relatively free and fluid economy. The profit system has its faults, but it has been a creator of wealth and initiative, and I hope that we will be able to preserve it in its essentials even as we try to alleviate the injustices of history. I like the freedom of choice that does exist, and I like the determination of the American people to try, where possible, to broaden that freedom. I do not agree with those 18th Century philosophers who felt that every civil right is, at root, a property right, but I do believe we have to be free to make economic choices, or we are not free at all.

In the wake of Vietnam and Watergate, I think I may be most grateful for the stubborn and at times even touchingly naive idealism of the American people. We do wash our dirty linen in public. We do wrestle with our consciences. We do search the Constitution and the law for firm guides to public conduct.

Watergate, in particular, seemed to me to show the American Republic at its most resilient. The betrayal of trust was confronted, calmly and systematically, but the country kept its composure and kept its head. I was and am proud of that. Corruption is challenged. The country maintains a corporate sense of decency and the fitness of things.

There are many things wrong with the country, to be sure, and we should not forget them. The line I have always liked best in "America the Beautiful" is the one about "mend thine every flaw." In an imperfect world, we are imperfect, too. Our tax system is flawed. Racial injustices persist. Economic injustices abound. Our attention span for long-term problems is too short. Some of our institutions, as for instance the criminal justice system, don't work right. There is too little emphasis on civility and honesty and mutual respect. We accept celluloid definitions of what constitutes the good life.

But we know those things, and we work at them. We know that America is always in the process of becoming. We know, even in our deep-rooted and old-fashioned idealism, that there is no such thing as the perfect republic or the absolutely secure and just society. We know that we have enjoyed many of the blessings of history through no particular virtue of our own and that we have to struggle on to build on them and to turn them to our advantage, and to humanity's.

I have three children of my own. I do not pity them as they come of age in America's third century. They will have problems, just as we have had and will have.

Nonetheless, there is much here to build a life with: opportunity, tradition, stability, ideals, strength.

Such blessings are probably about the most that any people ever had the right to ask of history and their forebears.

And they are certainly enough to make me, on this day, glad to be a part of what America has tried to be in the world.

And glad, too, to be around for the start of the Republic's third century.

Toward a more Democratic Party

New York — When Barbara Jordan delivered her keynote address to the Democratic convention Monday night, a lot of history was telescoped before us.

As she spoke, my eyes turned over to my left from the press gallery to the delegation from my native state of Arkansas. Blacks and whites together.

To Georgia, the home state of the apparent nominee, the place where Sherman's troops marched through. Blacks and whites together. To Alabama, the state in which George Wallace stood in the schoolhouse door to keep black children out. Blacks and whites together.

As I looked out over that scene, as I heard Barbara Jordan speak in that elegant, rolling voice that was created for convention halls, I thought of other conventions, other times.

I remembered sitting by the radio in 1948, listening to the fight for civil rights, to the beginning of the Dixiecrats' revolt of that year. I remember leafing through the little yellow-covered handbook that was my father's guide to the laws of the state Democratic Party and finding there the vestiges of the white primary, of the discriminatory use of the poll tax.

JULY 14, 1976

Now, the Democratic Party wears its pluralism with far more grace, more ease. A Southern white nominee who gets black votes. A black keynoter saluted by "The Eyes of Texas."

At that age — 12 — I did not understand all of that fully. But now I cannot help but share Congresswoman Jordan's exultation that she could stand before that convention this week, in that capacity, and speak to the heart and conscience of America. Those who seek their high drama in numbers and suspense and conflict may have missed the significance of that moment, and of how far we have come.

It is easy, this year, to mock the McGovern convention of 1972, with its crude quota democracy, its collection of minorities strung together by rules. In that convention, though, was a battering ram that broke down many of the vestiges of racism in the Democratic Parties of the states.

Now, the Democratic Party wears its pluralism with far more grace, more ease. It may not be a true democracy yet, but it is getting there. A Southern white nominee who gets black votes. A black keynoter saluted by "The Eyes of Texas." Women who can legitimately claim a victory for feminism while having lost their request for strict numerical quotas.

This is important, and I believe now such factors will be permanent if hereafter less and less remarkable. It should not pass unremarked by the leaders of the Republican Party, the party of Lincoln.

In Michigan, Bill Milliken has tried to tell the Republican Party that it must reach out more effectively to the young, the black, the diverse. It is a somber truth.

The vision of American society held by many Republicans is not inherently anti-black, or anti-city, or anti-working man, but in recent years much of the GOP's preachment and practice has seemed that way. If the Republicans are not going to be forever a minority party, they must find ways to reach out, to broaden themselves, to speak within their party doctrines to the diversity of America.

As Congresswoman Jordan spoke Monday night, she invoked the name of Abraham Lincoln. How ironic, I thought. What a mistake the Republicans made in 1876, when they compromised away the first Reconstruction. For the sake of a disputed presidential election they compromised with the racism of the Old South.

Now, 100 years later, the Democratic Party, after all the years of convulsions and struggle, is putting together its coalition again. America's appetite for change is, I suspect, fairly limited now. Its vision of itself, after all the years of tumult, may even be essentially conservative. Even though there is an awareness of flaws, many Americans believe they have much to hang on to.

But we shouldn't lose sight, after we look back on the upheaval of the '60s and early '70s and on the pain of those years, that the changes had to come and that the country's prospects are better for their having come.

There were and are side effects, to be sure: a loss of order, a decline of restraint, a sense of disquiet.

Yet Monday night the cheering multitude in New York heard a black congresswoman tell them that her presence was in itself a reassurance that the American dream need not be "forever deferred."

It was a remarkable event.

Without Ford, we'd be worse off

Reading now the generous tributes he is receiving in the press, Gerald Ford is entitled to ask where all these friendly voices were last November, when he needed them.

President Ford has, in fact, enjoyed a pretty good press all along, even among people who did not wind up supporting him last November. Largely that is a result of his personal qualities, rather than his ideology or his intellect.

I believed last November and feel it even more strongly now that it was right for the country to make a change, that the policies of the administration would not suffice for the long pull, that the vision of America that Jimmy Carter projected seemed to have more to do with the realities in the country as I see them.

And yet as the torch passes this week from Gerald Ford to Jimmy Carter, I feel, as most Americans do, a sense of special appreciation for Gerald Ford and what he has contributed to the country over a lifetime of public service, and especially over the past 30 months.

He was, in an even more valid sense than Lyndon Johnson, an "accidental president." If I had been asked five years ago to name the best Michigan Republican prospects for the presidency, he would have been perhaps third on the list. He did not seem to be a man born to be president.

Though he was for years the minority leader in the House of Representatives,

Jan. 16, 1977

Without Gerald Ford's stability of character and his sense of what is right and appropriate, the country might have been through far more trouble and might be now handed over to President Carter in worse shape.

he had not shone through as a strong personality. Where was the monumental legislation? Where was the response to crisis or the bold act? To tell the truth, I was surprised at many aspects of Gerald Ford's personality as it emerged in the White House. There was more warmth than I had expected, less of a partisan edge, more subtlety, and at a personal level, more of a feeling for people. And in many ways, the most appealing part of his personality has been his wholeness, his lack of inner tension, his easiness in human relations.

By the end of his 30 months in the White House, Gerald Ford had pretty clearly decided he liked being president, or so I sense. The loss in November may not have driven him into a shell, as Newsweek reported soon after and the White House denied. Plainly, though, he was disappointed.

It is small consolation, too, to know the odds that were against him, to remember what the Democratic Convention in New York was like, to think what the spirits of Republicans were like at Kansas City, and to reflect on how close a race it became. Jerry Ford wanted to win, and he didn't.

But there should be consolation for Mr. Ford and for those partisans who fought and bled for him in knowing how much his interim presidency contributed to the life of this country. True, he leaves an agenda with many of the big questions barely touched: the problem of energy scarcity and price, the opening up of new and deeper class divisions in parts of the American society, the crisis of the cities, now approaching new depths.

When Mr. Ford took office, though, the lion was in the streets. Richard Nixon, whose lack of security was every bit as manifest as Gerald Ford's serenity is, had left the presidency crippled and beset. The loss of faith was profound; the sense of frustration was deep; the lack of direction and self-respect was corrosive.

Gerald Ford did not change all that single-handedly. Congress helped, even though it is much maligned and even though some of its members disgraced themselves. A healthy, open and relatively lively campaign was in itself something of a catharsis. Mostly, it was the American people themselves who, with all their faults, possess a strength and basic hopefulness that have stood up under heavy pressures these last few years.

Jimmy Carter may well turn out to be both a product of and a contributor to that continuing catharsis. A few of his appointments seem more dubious to me than I would have hoped. His economic program may not be adequate. But basically I feel pretty good about the sense of steadiness and competence that he evokes. Still, without Gerald Ford's stability of character and his sense of what is right and appropriate, the country might have been through far more trouble and might be now handed over to President Carter in worse shape. For that, we can all be grateful. It is hard to imagine Gerald Ford in the role of retiree or elder statesman. He has many qualities that might be useful to his country, to his party, or even to a president elected from the other party. We hope he will find, or be given, outlets for his energies, his talents and his love of country. He does have something to contribute.

And especially for us in Michigan, including those of us who supported his victorious opponent last November, there is an abiding sense that this was and is a solid, straightforward man who saw a duty and did it. A man whose country is better off today because he was there, because of what he is and what he isn't.

Women search for a new integrity

It is a mistake, I suspect, to speak of "the women's movement."

To do so tends to evoke images of militant feminists, burning their bras, overturning the tables in the locker room and sometimes in the temple, overemphasizing lesbian rights and abortion, alienating men and often other women.

All those things have been, at one time or another, a part of the pattern of the protests about the legal and actual status of women. As in most of the currents of opinion that surge, from time to time, through the body politic, "the women's movement" has had in its forefront the angry and the alienated. They are almost always the stuff of which revolutions are made.

JULY 13, 1978

Contrary to the stereotypes, a great many women are trying to preserve old values as they seek new arrangements.

The real importance of the women's movement, however, is that what is happening with women in America is much more fundamental and significant than a simple political movement.

At some point the historians and the sociologists will be able to explain, in a way we can understand, the earthquake in attitudes and concern that has shaken so many American households and has reshaped so many relationships. It is difficult to define what has happened simply in terms of issues. The assertion that there is a uniformity of women's opinions is a patronizing disservice.

But something basic has been happening. Part of it is that enough women work outside the home these days and have done it long enough that they know they are persons in their own right. Part of it is that our consciousness is constantly raised by the recurrent reminders that, in the shaping of our attitudes, it has been "a man's world."

Part of it is simply that many families today are small enough, and affluent enough, and literate enough, that there is an inevitable questioning of roles and practices and societal structures.

I do not claim to be a liberated male, in the sense of understanding all of what is happening to women and their attitudes, or of being in tune with it. In many ways, I am and always will be a small-town Southern boy with peasant tastes and comprehension. But I do sense that there is in the anguished cry of many of today's women a protest as irresistible and inevitable as any other we have seen in recent years.

I know, too, that one reason my brothers and I are all newspapermen is that, as high school students in Arkansas, we fell under the influence of a remarkable weekly newspaper editor, Charlotte Schexnayder, now editor of the Dumas, Ark., Clarion and president of the National Press Women's Organization. Thirty years ago, she liberated her own talent and helped us to liberate ours.

So maybe I had a personal reason to know of the contributions women can make, not in their traditional roles alone, but in what were once men-only preserves.

From homebodies who chose that lot and love it, to career women with barely enough time in their lives for a family, to painfully conscientious persons who balance the two options in their lives, there is a searching for a new significance, a new integrity, a new place in the world.

Some of the effect, as with any social convulsion, has been bad. There is a lot of confusion. There is conflict. There are responsibilities that are sometimes going unmet. There is a lot of guilt about clashing roles.

Nonetheless, there is an excitement that I find impressive and interesting. Contrary to the stereotypes, a great many women are trying to preserve old values as they seek new arrangements. And they are — or so it seems to me — as divided and unsure of where their new self-awareness is taking them as any other human group would be dealing with such dynamic forces.

The social forces involved are incredibly complex and yet so personal and direct that they touch the lives of virtually every one of us.

Carter: A moment to exult, a job to face

When Prime Minister Menachem Begin added his endorsement to President Anwar Sadat's description of Jimmy Carter as the "unknown soldier" of the peace process during the Monday ceremonies — saying, "I agree, but as usual, with an amendment" — President Carter could be heard, off-camera, almost exploding with laughter.

His enjoyment of the occasion and his pride in the treaty were almost touching in their unabashedness. It was a moment to be savored, and he was savoring it. And for a man who has not had that much to smile about in recent months, here was a time to laugh out loud.

MARCH 28, 1979

Polls in the United States and protests in the Middle East and elsewhere showed what the president had to know: that such moments are always endangered, that even the most genuine achievements often seem pallid after they have been accomplished and that these treaties can be counted as no more than a beginning.

We must hope Carter can be as persuasive with the American masses as he is with the heads of alienated states.

With all the protests, with all the polls showing the lack of impact on domestic politics, the achievement seems to me to be real and important and its potential contribution to the peace of the world is more fundamental than one might believe, listening to the protesters.

It is only a cornerstone, and a cornerstone cannot suffice as a structure for peace. And when one considers the labor that went into bringing just this achievement about, and how nettlesome the problems that remain in the Middle East alone, one has to wonder whether Mr. Carter will be able to see it through, or whether he will have time for the other accumulated problems of his presidency if he does try to see it through. Still, this achievement matters.

Mr. Carter brought about this treaty by dealing from his strengths: tenacity, faith, mastery of detail, personal persuasiveness. Those strengths have not projected well in the public arena. In the matter of style, Mr. Carter often has failed, since the shining moment of his Inaugural Day walk, to understand the importance of symbols and of mass communications.

It has been a strange void. His presidential campaign was laden with symbolism. He seemed, almost intuitively, to understand the sort of hunger in the country's soul for some new framework for dealing with its problems, for some new sense of where it was going and what it has always been.

Mr. Carter's approach to problems has often seemed almost mechanical: that there is a right and logical answer to things, and that his role as leader has been to stay at the task until he worked out those details in a way that was so logical and compelling that people would accept his view. And far from building consensus, he seemed often to swing from arbitrariness to compromise.

The cliché — that his is almost a systems approach, an engineer's approach — is not entirely wrong. And unfortunately he has not had the level of competence on his staff and in his cabinet to carry out that sort of coolly rational approach. In a mediation setting, where he personally could deal with the detail, Mr. Carter could do very well. But the rationalism he projects at close quarters does not come through in a State of the Union speech.

It may be asking too much to hope that Jimmy Carter will change, that he will understand the essence of leadership that involves showmanship. Mr. Carter sometimes seems to operate on the premise that leadership is a science. John Kennedy, or even Lyndon Johnson, or Henry Kissinger could have told him that it is in considerable measure simply theater — understanding drama and human emotion, pulling people together, setting collective goals.

I personally like Mr. Carter's style better than most people do. The record of his administration — even if it should turn out to be only a one-term administration — may show more real achievement than most are inclined to give him credit for at this time.

To say that, however, is not to ignore the deep and pervasive question about Mr. Carter's presidency: Can he identify for us and convince us about the program that will let us respond to the basic issues of our time? Can he convey a sense of a sure hand on the wheel?

And while we may laugh and exult with him at the genuine achievement he wrought this week, we must hope that he can understand the awesome tone-setting power of the office he holds. We must hope he can be as persuasive with the American masses as he is with the heads of alienated states.

There are things about Mr. Carter that we may be able only to accept: his stubbornness, his unorthodox style of approaching issues, a sometime appearance of naivete about his approach to legislative strategy.

But there are things about presidential leadership that he must accept, too: that the White House is indeed a bully pulpit and that the president who fails to use it to give his people a vision of themselves, as well as to lead the heads of other states, has failed to exploit the true power and the opportunity of his office.

A father's letter to a draft-age son

Dear Son,

As I drove home alone from seeing you at the university on Saturday, I found myself deep in thought — about you, about the good day we had had together, about the world situation, about the draft.

I'm not sure you understood what I was trying to say as I left you at your dorm. Probably you did. You seem remarkably able to understand what I say, even when it is something mushy and fatherly like "You're a source of a lot of joy to me."

In any case, I was touched, in my conversations with you and your friends, by the struggling that college-age people are going through now over the draft issue. I am frustrated that the country's actions, in the wake of the Soviet Union's invasion of Afghanistan, seem not to have been very well understood or very well explained.

When I read or hear of university students shouting, "We won't go for Texaco," or arguing that the country is asking them to trade blood for oil, I know that the president has not succeeded in explaining to people why our "vital interests" are involved in the Persian Gulf.

FEB. 15, 1980

If we react with some firmness and clarity, I think that the Soviets and not the United States may emerge the losers. Maybe they already have. They are paying a price for their assault on their helpless neighbor.

You know, I think, that I do not want you to have to go to war, ever, for any reason. I would worry the long nights away. You know I am a worrier where you and your sisters are concerned. You know your mother and I will hold our breath worrying about your liability for the draft, even.

And I certainly would not want you to have to die to protect our inalienable right to drive a big car, or overheat our house, or even to preserve our standard of living. We would trade the amenities in a minute if that were what was at stake.

But it isn't just the amenities that are at issue here. Even under the wisest conservation policies in the world, the need in the world for access to that oil is going to remain. More than that, aggression of such naked force is a threat to all of us, anywhere in the world.

My government — your government — has not done well enough at mobilizing the country to reduce our vulnerability by cutting our dependence on the Persian Gulf oil. If anything were to happen to you because of our lack of discipline as a country, I would be mad as the dickens. The country has to do better than it has done at reducing our dependence on that vulnerable lifeline, and it has to do it quick.

So, no, I don't want you to be drafted to fight for American energy dependence.

To tell you the truth, I believe that it may not be necessary for any young Americans to be drafted soon or to die. The response to the Soviets' naked aggression must have surprised them. The Muslim countries, the United States, even India now — what the Soviets are getting is not the sort of flabby acquiescence they might have expected, though there has been some of that. The United States and indeed the world are challenging the Soviet Union's policy, despite what the International Olympic Committee has done.

For the most part — despite some reckless talk by representatives of the administration and others — it does not seem to be war fever or overreaction. I know many people think there has been overreaction. But I'm inclined to think we had no choice but to respond strongly, to invoke what weapons we had, to rally world opinion as best we could, to strengthen our ability to counter conventional military aggression, to make it clear the Soviet aggression does bear a price.

If we react with some firmness and clarity, I think that the Soviets and not the United States may emerge the losers. Maybe they already have. They are paying a price for their assault on their helpless neighbor.

I hope not only that what we are seeing does not foreshadow a hot war or even a return to the old Cold War. Détente never was, or at least never should have been, based on trust. I believe in cooperating where mutual interests say we can cooperate, and when the circumstances permit. Never should we have been naive in our approach to arms control, or whatever.

The next few months will be a delicate period. We could indeed get caught up in a new national fever. Or we could be plunged back to 1968, with people, especially young people, unable to see any difference between what we are trying to do now and what we tried to do in Vietnam. We could have a messy debate over the draft that would leave us more vulnerable and more paralyzed in the face of aggression rather than less.

You will make up your own mind and do your own thinking and come to your own conclusions. Your perspective may be different from mine. Heaven knows, the stakes are high, and I would be haunted all my life if my instincts proved wrong and you were sacrificed in some foolish military adventure of our own. I'm not sure your mother or I could survive that.

Even if there were no oil dependence, though, even if we could again be self-sufficient in terms of resources, I believe the country would have to be responding with some acts of firmness and will. Surely the lesson of Vietnam was not that we can only acquiesce when there is aggression, or that we should return to some Fortress America concept. The balance of power matters. The deterrence of aggression matters.

It won't mean world war, we have to hope. It won't and shouldn't necessarily mean that American troops will ever be directly involved. Quite possibly, it won't even mean that the draft will have to be activated, even though registration goes forward.

But it might. The world is in a risky situation now. It is a time for great caution and care, as well as for firmness and will. The lives of your generation, and maybe of all of us, are involved. I cannot write or think of the world situation without seeing the faces of you and your friends.

That doesn't tell you what to think or do. It doesn't even tell me what to think or do.

All it tells me is what is at stake in all these world events now.

And what is at stake is a son who will turn 20 this summer and who matters more to me than I can possibly say as he struggles with a world that now seems more threatening than before.

In other words, everything is at stake.

Love, Dad

A farming father knew bad years come, too

There by the barn, where the pungent smells of the farm made it seem a man's world, he talked about his dreams.

His dreams were for himself, for the farm, for me. They were buoyed up on a flood of rising expectations.

"Plastics," the graduate of the middle '60s was told. "The farm," my father said to his 10-year-old son in 1946.

The war that had consumed the world was over. In its wake was a society not so governed by illusion anymore; the world was plainly not safe for democracy. But it was a time governed by hope and expectation.

He was not a talkative man, but the subject of the world then unfolding made him talkative. He could excite the fancies of a son as he grew eloquent.

I did not know it then, but his rising expectations were a reflection of the country's. There was a world to be fed, to be rebuilt. There were possibilities to be explored.

MAY 11, 1980

Are they gone forever, those golden years of hope and promise? Certainly the easy hopes and cheap promises.

"Do it with me, son," his manner said. Let's build this postwar world together.

Off in Detroit, then, though I did not know it, there was the rush to rebuild the automobile industry for this car-starved country. I remember his jokes with friends and neighbors as cars began to be available again about the comparative virtues of a Chevrolet vs. a Ford or a Dodge.

The cities were teeming then — Detroit topped two million at one point — with people who crowded in to help build those cars and meet the other needs of postwar America. A time of beginnings it was: delayed beginnings for veterans. Pent-up beginnings for many whose lives had been depressed by the Great Crash and the war.

This was the time that shaped us, most of us now in mid-life. It was a world, always, of hope and aspiration and expectation.

That time did not prepare us for the '80s — not for a time when inflation is near 20 percent and recession is rampant, when power is limited and resources are too often controlled by other than Americans.

Our cities are full of school buildings and church buildings that are monuments to the inflated expectations of our generation. The countryside is sprawled with houses built in an era of cheap energy and cheap housing. Our heads are cluttered with the wreckage of dreams built on the notion of limitless growth and soaring optimism.

Now we see our friends and neighbors struggling with the shock waves that have swept across the automobile industry: workers suddenly thrust on one or another public dole; executives cut down in mid-career by sudden corporate crises.

My father knew that the good years after the war were always vulnerable, but I guess I didn't, at least not fully. Hope, the postwar years taught me. Tomorrow will be better.

Other people, elsewhere in the world, were not so naive about those years. They knew what they and their parents had suffered, and they had a longer struggle back to the good life.

Are they gone forever, those golden years of hope and promise? Certainly the easy hopes and cheap promises. There is no more cheap oil, cheap food, cheap housing. And government is too heavily obligated to be the deliverer. No simple change — such as rural electrification, or drainage, or a new road, or revenue sharing — will offer us easy salvation.

Facing that reality, we grow angry and frustrated. Who has failed us, we demand to know? Who has betrayed our dreams?

Yet it seems clear to me that, however much we believe is lost in America in 1980, the fault is not in the stars but in ourselves: in our failure to understand what discipline and dedication and daring are asked of us.

That is not an easy thing to know or to say. I am working; some are not. How can I dare to speak of discipline and demands? How can anyone frustrate the dreams and trifle with the expectations of those now commencing their lives?

Plainly, though, we will not open the doors and the possibilities and rebuild the dreams just by wishing. Our society has to change. Our children do, and we do. I believe we can.

It seemed easier then, listening to Dad there by the barn. But we are living now, after better times, fulfilled hopes. And it is important for us to go on building now. It can't be a world of easy promise anymore. But it can, I think, be a world of promise again.

Democracy can lose to cynicism, apathy

That night in 1960 was one my idealism had not prepared me to face.

It was primary night in Arkansas, in the summer our son was born, in the year of my brief involvement in politics.

To describe what happened, I need to supply a bit of personal background.

I had come out of graduate school in 1959 with fire in my eyes and the sense that political change had to come and come quickly. The South was in the midst of the civil rights turmoil then, and back home in Arkansas, Orval Faubus had used the race issue to fashion a political machine the likes of which the state had never seen.

When I left home in 1957, I had planned to be a history teacher in a small college, an ambition inspired by a favorite professor from my undergraduate years. By the middle of the 1958-59 school year, I could stand it no more. How could I rehash the causes of World War I when a revolution was happening back home, when people were debating basic issues such as the survival of the public schools, and racial justice and even free speech?

SEPT. 21, 1980

It seems almost a sacrilege to decide nothing matters, that candidates and principles and even thin margins of difference between people are unimportant.

Harry Ashmore was winning Pulitzer Prizes for his editorials in the Arkansas Gazette in Little Rock at the time, and I decided what I most wanted to do in the world was to be an editorial writer, to try to address the great issues of the day. I had apprenticed on my hometown newspaper as a teenager, so it was not a strange idea, but I had resisted the idea until I witnessed the courage of some of the Southern editors of the day. Somehow I had to go back home and do what I thought was right about helping my native state undo the mess it was in.

A year after I entered newspapering, I was asked to work as a press secretary to the leading opposition candidate for governor. The paper I was working for gave me a leave, my wife said she thought I should do it, and I plunged that summer of 1960 into 18- and 20-hour days. The candidate, Joe Hardin, was a good and decent man but a rather poor candidate, and I had more conviction than political insight.

But I began to write speeches for him, and the conviction grew in me that somehow, against all those horrible odds, we could bring it off. We didn't. The array of forces supporting the incumbent governor was simply too powerful.

The night we lost is one that is forever seared in memory. We were not surprised, but we were deeply disappointed. And I remember wondering whether the system worked, whether it was possible to bring about change, whether you could have an impact. My wife had even cleverly arranged for our son to be born on a July Sunday morning two weeks before the primary; if it had been any other day, I might not even have been able to get there in time. It was a time of intense political commitment.

And it had been for naught. The system had prevailed. The cynics and the bosses had won.

That summer of 1960 comes back to mind as I hear people say now that politics doesn't matter, that nothing changes, that there aren't real choices. I have even had letters from young people saying we should boycott the system because the system doesn't work.

I think I know the despair they feel, though I cannot endorse the disdain for the system or for political effort and commitment.

Of course, that summer's effort really turned out not to be for naught. Joe Hardin lost, but his speaking up for the preservation of a strong public school system and for opposition to the haters began to have an effect. He helped in a small way to prepare the way for what happened later in that Southern state, with Winthrop Rockefeller and later Dale Bumpers and a continuing series of progressive, antiracist governors and the breakup of the old regime.

Last week, the Free Press' excellent political writer, Remer Tyson, brought me the text of the presidential debates of 1960 between Richard Nixon and John Kennedy. He had come across it again, he said, and it seemed to him that parts of it showed that political debate and rhetoric do sometimes matter.

It would be difficult to excerpt the material from even the first, crucial debate in any way that would be both coherent and readable. Much of it seems dated now, though much of it does not. The rhetoric of John Kennedy in particular seems almost prophetic.

In just one area — the area that was the focus of so much of our lives that election year in Arkansas, the issue of civil rights — Sen. Kennedy had begun to call us to our duty.

"I'm not satisfied," Sen. Kennedy said, "until every American enjoys his full constitutional rights. If a Negro baby is born, and this is true also of Puerto Ricans and Mexicans in some of our cities, he has about one-half as much chance to get through high school as a white baby. He has one-third as much chance to get through college as a white student. He has about a third as much chance to be a professional man, and about half as much chance to own a house. He has about four times as much chance that he'll be out of work in his life as the white baby. I think we can do better. I don't want the talents of any American to go to waste."

To read those words now is to realize both how much has been done and how little, how much the agenda has changed and how much it has remained the same. They were not especially bold words, but they identified, in human terms, an important part of the nation's agenda.

The system often does not respond, even to our personal moral imperatives. It often gets bogged down in cynicism and apathy and irrelevance.

Still, it seems to me almost a sacrilege to decide nothing matters, that candidates and principles and even thin margins of difference between people are unimportant.

It is not easy for us to translate our personal ideals into societal policy, whatever those ideals are. How, though, can we ever spurn the struggle?

The utopias, the ultimate answers, will always elude us. The struggle is always there. The foremost political crime of this or any season is giving way to despair.

Jimmy Carter: The man we never knew

For most people, Jimmy Carter was and is a person who could never pass the bus-station test.

The bus-station test, a friend of mine in North Carolina used to say, is the ultimate: If you had to sit up all night in a bus station, whom could you tolerate as a companion? It is a stern test.

From the first time I met Jimmy and Rosalynn Carter, back in 1974, I wondered about them and that test. At a banquet of the American Society of Newspaper Editors meeting in Atlanta, I sat by her. He was across the table. I liked Rosalynn then and like her now. We talked of Georgia, of race and changes in the South. I found her smart and tough. I did not think then of "the steel magnolia" — someone pinned that label on her later — but in retrospect it fit.

Always, there was something so relentlessly purposeful about both of them, though: discipline, dedication, intelligence, a sort of cunning shrewdness. I have always wondered what the inner person was like, in both cases.

Nov. 9, 1980

Jimmy Carter has understood a lot about symbolism, enough to be elected to the highest office in this land. But he never really mastered the role of charismatic leader.

Washington and the country have consistently wondered that, too. Jimmy Carter probably spent less time than any other president on building the little human ties that are the glue of politics. Jerry Ford was exceptionally good at that; Richard Nixon was not good at it but did work at it; Lyndon Johnson was magnificent at it.

Television and film have sharpened the gap between public image and private reality for many personalities. The warmth, the humor, the mimicry, the self-mocking coarseness, the manipulative shrewdness and, yes, the West Texas idealism that made Lyndon Johnson such a delight over drinks never translated on television. And when he reaped the whirlwind over Vietnam, Lyndon Johnson's persuasive talents as a private person could not hold for him the constituency he really needed, namely, the people who knew him only as a strange-talking, overbearing, public personality.

Jimmy Carter has understood a lot about symbolism, enough to be elected to the highest office in this land, and there have been times, rare times, when as president he communicated very well. But he never really mastered the role of charismatic leader, and he was so private, so mechanical and introverted, that he did not inspire, save in that little band of Georgia faithful around him, the intense kind of personal feeling that can sustain a public man through difficult times.

One of the interesting things to watch about Jimmy Carter over the next few years is what this defeat will do to him. It is a matter of purely clinical interest, of course; Jimmy Carter will not be back, though the years may be kinder to him and his record than the harsh judgments of this fall have been.

In defeat, moreover, we may eventually begin to understand better the enigma that he represents. I thought his concession statement was revealing and graceful. I liked him better in that moment than I ever did in happier times. There was warmth in it, and serenity.

In small-group settings, I have found the president philosophical and intelligent, reflective and compassionate. The supposed meanness of spirit has not come through to me in such contexts, though its existence has certainly shown up in his campaigns.

Unlike many of the people who covered his campaigns and his White House, I have genuinely liked Jimmy Carter as a human being, though I cannot say I ever truly understood him. I think the country may eventually come to like him better and maybe to know him better in retirement.

These human-level questions matter less, of course, than the great questions of philosophy and policy. Yet the presidency is a very personal office, and we tend to see the people who occupy it in very human terms. And I cannot easily lay aside the question of the president as a person.

What the country will remember now is the colossal defeat, the first elected president defeated after one term since Herbert Hoover. That is important. But a person can be president of the United States only two terms at most. Jimmy Carter made it there, against all odds, for one. For a boy from Plains, Ga. — for a boy from anywhere — that achievement is remarkable enough.

At the human level, I am sad for Jimmy Carter now. The missed opportunities will haunt him for the rest of his life. The failures will be troubling.

Most of all, though, I am sad that he did not let us — the country, all of us — know him better. I think he might very well be all right in a bus-station vigil. Maybe far more than all right.

Sadly, though, we still don't know for sure.

Maybe we never will.

Listen to the cries of the poor

They were mostly not the poor themselves, but they were people who work with and for the poor, and they gave vent to some frustrations with the media.

Their opportunity came at a Lansing meeting of the Michigan League for Human Services, in a workshop where several of us from newspapers and television appeared to talk about how to deal with the media.

They asked hard questions: How do the poor gain access to the media to express their points of view? What about situations in various towns in Michigan where there is monopoly ownership of the newspapers? What do you do when you feel you have been wronged by a newspaper or television? Is there a conspiracy to keep certain viewpoints out of the paper? To what extent is the political bias of a paper evident in its news columns?

The question of access to the media is a tough one. We are in the business of allocating limited space — or, in the case of television and radio, air time — and

APRIL 12, 1981

There is a danger that we are hearing only what we think we want to hear, that we are ignoring, once again, the rumble of the distant drum of social discontent.

there is tremendous power in that judgment. The worst danger may not be the deliberate misrepresentation or the inadvertent mistake, but the fact that there is a threshold below which something is not news and above which it is. How do we decide when an issue becomes news, or warrants the Legislature's attention, or deserves to be a national priority?

We have to make the editorial judgments, because people can and will read only selectively. Their time is limited. They want information organized and presented intelligibly. Indeed, they are drowning in words as it is; they want help in establishing significance. And yet the power to gauge significance — to make news and editorial judgments — is an awesome power.

The truth is, of course, that we always do see, in St. Paul's language, "through a glass darkly." The media did not tell the story of the emerging crisis in American cities in the mid-'60s early enough or well enough. We did not recognize the Vietnam War's impact on the country, and television's impact on Vietnam, early enough or well enough. We did not — most of us, anyhow — recognize early enough or well enough the moral rot that led to Watergate. We did not sense the full potential of the Reagan counterrevolution early enough or well enough. And in general, it seems to me, we are not now fully capturing the extent of the changes the Reagan administration is making in American life.

So, yes, our human judgments, however defensible on a given day, often add up to a cumulative misjudgment about the direction and significance of trends in our society. And yes, those forces in society that we most often overlook are those centered in the parts of the population that are rendered voiceless or inarticulate. Sometimes it is the middle class; more often it is the poor.

I worry now about the voicelessness of the poor in the midst of the counterrevolution going on in America. Congress can cut social programs and raise defense spending, and the protests may well continue to be muddled, as indeed they are now. But does that mean there is not needless pain? We can cut CETA (Comprehensive Employment and Training Act) jobs and say we are promoting self-sufficiency, but will we really encourage independence and self-sufficiency?

Or are we now moving systematically to create a permanent underclass, stranded in the old Frost Belt cities, with no visible prospects for jobs, an educational system that still falls far short of meeting its obligations, an industrial society that is increasingly relying on robots, an economy that is failing to generate a sufficient number of new jobs? And if we are, is there a danger that, one or two summers from now, we will begin to face renewed civil strife in our cities, renewed frustration from the poor and the powerless?

I honestly don't know for certain. I hope the president is right about the effect of his economic strategy, though I am skeptical. I hope the truly needy are being protected. I hope renewed economic stimulation can produce new industrial growth, new jobs, new wealth to meet the needs of the people.

But it seems to me there is a danger that we are hearing only what we think we want to hear, that we are ignoring, once again, the rumble of the distant drum of social discontent and that, in the name of economic policy, we are dismantling some of the means by which we have staved off disaster since the mid-'60s. We forgot to listen once before for those voices of discontent, and we regretted our ignorance and arrogance later on.

In Detroit, we dare not make that mistake again. Of course the country must deal with inflation. Of course it must find new ways to encourage investment. Of course it must foster such growth as the economy can reasonably support. Of course we must combat waste and fraud.

Let us not, though, fail to listen for those scattered cries of discontent, for those challenges to the new conservative consensus, for those who say there are dangers in the dismantling of so much of the human service apparatus built up over the last half century. We must listen and try to make sure our society — including the media — provides them access to power and to a voice in what is happening.

The point is in danger of being lost in the preoccupation with the winds of political change blowing in Washington. If it is brushed aside, though, there will be time enough for hindsight and regret, later on.

We dare not fail to listen, not again.

Women should have freedom to choose

For me, as I suspect for most people, the public policy question of freedom of choice for women is a lot easier to resolve than the private question of abortion.

Helen Milliken, the governor's wife, said recently following a speech on freedom of choice that she had never had an abortion and was not sure what she would do if she had to confront that question.

But on the issue of preserving the right to choose, she is absolutely unambiguous. It should be a woman's right.

How can a president and a Congress preoccupied with "getting government off our backs" argue that in the most intimate of decisions — whether to bear a child — the government should roll back the freedom of choice that now exists?

I yield to no one in my concern about the cheapening of life and the respect for life. I regard any taking of human life as grievous. It is a mistake to encourage the lessening of respect for life at any point on the spectrum.

The argument about whether the unborn fetus is the same as a person, however, without qualification or doubt, seems to me to fly in the face of legal history and reality. Do we feel the same about a miscarriage as we do about the death of a child? Is the prospective child at the moment of conception the same as the real child that we hold in our arms and love?

MAY 10, 1981

How can a president and a Congress preoccupied with "getting government off our backs" argue that in the most intimate of decisions — whether to bear a child — the government should roll back the freedom of choice that now exists?

All the efforts to determine scientifically the moment at which the fetus has some innate "right to life" seem destined to end in confusion and complexity. Does that "right to life" threaten the prospective mother's right to determine whether she bears a child? Does it mean that most forms of birth control are wrong?

For many people, many sincere people involved in the antiabortion movement, the answer is yes. They accept the teaching that interference in the divinely ordained process of reproduction by artificial means is wrong. They are as plainly against artificial birth control as against abortion. And for at least some, there is yet another leap: to opposition to any sex education.

A cousin who is a county health officer in a Western state tells me of finding himself and his county board the center of a right-to-life controversy. Why? Not because of the abortion issue. Not even over birth control device dispensation. What they had done was to provide to the public schools a limited program of sex education.

I am not sure how deep or how broad this body of opinion is. An educator in one of Detroit's northern suburbs tells me that when his school system provided a physical education/personal health program, with sex education and one without, only a bare handful of people opted to take their children out of the sex education program. Nonetheless, the vocal protests occur every time the issue is to be raised.

A decision to have or not to have an abortion does involve a collision of rights: the right of the mother to make her own decision about what happens to her body, the right of the unborn to be protected by law at least at some point in the process of being born. There is nothing approaching a consensus about how to reconcile that conflict.

That fact — the diversity of views on the question of abortion — would seem to argue that the decision ought to be a matter of individual conscience within broad limits. Individual freedom would seem better served by keeping the state out of this matter.

The Hyde Amendment argument — whether the government should pay for abortions for people eligible for Medicaid — has skewed the issue somewhat. Without Medicaid payments, many poor women would be and are denied access to legal abortions and therefore have the decision made for them by the state. But many people who can accept the fact that abortion should be a matter for private decision are troubled by the concept of the government's paying for something about which they personally have problems of conscience.

As long as Medicaid is, in effect, the health insurance for a significant part of the population, it would seem to me an intolerable double standard to deny funding for abortions for the poor while the more affluent have the right to choose. So I support Medicaid payments for abortion for those women who are eligible for Medicaid and who choose abortion.

That argument over government funding, though, should not obscure the larger issue: whether the right to choose will be preserved. And at a time when the president and Congress are moving to deregulate business, they should not be permitted to intrude themselves into the private decisions of multitudes of women across this country.

Mondale breaks a significant barrier

Until Thursday, there wasn't much about the 1984 presidential campaign that I would have wanted to put in my scrapbook.

In announcing that Geraldine Ferraro will be his running mate, Walter Mondale gave us something to remember in American political history. I wish I had been at the Minnesota State House. Whatever happens in the campaign, that was — as the Wall Street Journal described it — an electric moment.

The act of choosing her means more than I had anticipated. It does not necessarily, in and of itself, mean Walter Mondale is back in the race. It will help him because it will energize an important set of troops. But he faces formidable problems, many of his own making. He is going to have to solve them.

JULY 15, 1984

Another barrier was pulled down and demolished. There is now a whole new set of folks who feel the process is open to them.

What the Ferraro appointment does suggest, though, is that good ol' Walter — bland, dull, Deputy Dawg Walter — has some sense of theater and of history, too.

The right kind of theater can make a campaign. Remember the rolling thunder of Barbara Jordan at the 1976 Democratic Convention and the tearful, joyful closing session with Jimmy Carter and Daddy King joined in joyous embrace and the crowd singing "We Shall Overcome"? Those two seemingly redemptive moments infused the Carter campaign of that year with some sense of moral purpose.

Dwight Eisenhower was not credited with much sense of political theater, but that was almost certainly wrong. On the one hand, he somehow conveyed that sense of being above the battle. On the other, the cries of "I like Ike" conveyed a warmth that made him human, especially when we saw the famous grin responding.

John Kennedy may have understood it best among American postwar presidents. Why is it I can still remember with such compelling force his confrontation, during the primary season, with the Baptist ministers of Houston? You knew in that moment that the old, evil anti-Catholic dictum about American presidential politics was dying. A single, dramatic moment of political theater had changed the rules of American politics. Good political theater can do that.

Bad theater, of course — the tear gas and the Chicago police in 1968 or the hard-eyed zealotry of some of the faces at the 1964 Republican convention — can stamp impressions so indelibly on the minds of people that a campaign can be won or lost on those images alone. A lot of Democrats had worried until now that the Democrats would let bad theater dominate the television screens this week from San Francisco.

Walter Mondale and Geraldine Ferraro changed all that on Thursday. He and she put the selection of her in precisely the right context: as an extension and an expansion of the American tradition. How could this be, as the ubiquitous Phyllis Schlafly sourly said in a television interview, Mondale's surrender to the "radical feminists"? There she stood — mother of three, wife of long standing, hardworking night law school graduate, product of an imigrant family.

Whatever else happens in this campaign of 1984, something deeply important happened in St. Paul last week. Another barrier was pulled down and demolished. There is now a whole new set of folks who feel the process is open to them. That's important.

I remember, as a 12-year-old Southern white boy listening to favorite-son nominations during the stormy 1948 Democratic convention and wondering why the Southerners weren't really a part of the main show. I must say it meant something to me later when, with first Lyndon Johnson and then Jimmy Carter, we got to the point where, as Southerners joked, we "had a president who didn't have an accent." I felt the process was more nearly my process.

I think I understand what it means to black people to see Jesse Jackson running right out there with everyone else, debating the issues with other politicians. I'm glad young black children have had the chance to see that happen this year. I hope we won't have to wait another generation before the perfectly logical thing to do is to put a black man or woman on the ticket.

Geraldine Ferraro, being human, will undoubtedly stumble at some point. Ms. Ferraro will carry a special burden. Pioneers almost always do. The country will demand more of her, as a candidate and conceivably as vice president, than she can possibly give.

It will help to break down barriers further if she succeeds admirably, of course. Maybe we — and she — will be lucky enough to have that happen.

For the moment, though, it is important and moving to know that Geraldine Ferraro is simply there. This country's democracy responds too slowly to the need to open itself up to broader participation. It is responding, though. And when the roll is called this week in San Francisco on the vice-presidential nomination, I'll be glad I'm there to see it. It will be a moment with real political meaning and promise.

A foolish war, an unfinished memorial

On a muggy, moonless Washington night a month or so ago, my wife and I caught a cab to the Lincoln Memorial area and went to see the new Vietnam Veterans Memorial.

Unfinished as the memorial is — with very poor lighting, an uneven walkway, a statue not yet in place — that is not the recommended time for a visit. Somehow, though, the dark shadows of the night, with martial music playing somewhere in the distance on the Mall, converted what might have been a tourist stop into almost a pilgrimage.

In the books that list the names of the dead in alphabetical order, protected from the elements by a plastic shield, we searched for the name of one of her classmates. She wanted to try to find his name on the black marble panels. The dead are listed chronologically on the panels. You have to go to the key and then count off the panels to locate the name of your brother, your lover, your friend.

JULY 29, 1984

It seemed typical of American ambiguity about that war to find the memorial deep in shadows, its walk not completed, its statue not yet finished.

As we arrived, there were a handful of people at the lowest point on the sloping walk beside the marble wall of panels, cigarette lighters flickering, searching the panels. "There he is," you could hear one of them say. Along the base of the wall, in the failing light, you could see flowers left to honor the dead.

Farther along the wall, away from the Lincoln Memorial, we encountered a man and woman with a small child and, in the camaraderie brought on by the eerie evening pilgrimage, talked with them, first about why there were so few lights and why the walk was already being reconstructed.

He was, it turned out, a veteran of that war. He spoke with rising anger about how long it had taken to build the memorial and how, even now, they still don't have it right. "They deserve better," he said, with a sweep of his arm toward the wall. "These guys deserve better."

As the darkness of the night continued to close in, we counted off, as best we could, the panels on the wall. We were never sure we were right, and in fact on that particular night could never locate the classmate's name. We counted and counted again, but somehow in the darkness could never get it right.

To me at least, though not to her, that seemed almost secondary. I did not know this particular young man. I was overwhelmed with the sense of how many young men were memorialized there, each one important to someone, each visitor searching for some way to put a particular death or a number of deaths into perspective, all of us wrestling with the moral ambiguities and the historical questions about that war.

It seemed typical of American ambiguity about that war to find the memorial deep in shadows, its walk not completed, its statue not yet finished, the names carved into the marble occasionally highlighted by the lights from the Mall.

I was glad that we as a country finally have begun to honor the dead, that the memorial honors the individual dead, that we have somehow been able to get far enough away from the dogmatism of the '60s to understand the pain and sadness and sacrifice of those men and women.

In the angry and bitter '60s, we told ourselves that this particular war was subject to an ambiguity that most others aren't, and that was partly true. Its purpose was even more obscure than most, its origins were more rooted in folly and ignorance about the history of a strange and remote place, the sacrifice it entailed was more dubious.

Wars, though, are almost always rooted in someone's folly, no matter how they may seem justified in the end. Even a war to destroy a known evil — e.g., a war to preserve the union or to destroy slavery — is at some level a result of the failure of less violent forms of statecraft. Wars, we have to tell ourselves, are at some level avoidable. There are ambiguities even at Gettysburg or Concord. There are young men who died because of a politician or a general who was stupid or vain or wasteful of human resources.

What we do, then, is memorialize those who died, not judge them or even ourselves. We go and search for them by a flickering light and sometimes find a name, sometimes not. We remember them as young boys, and we shudder at the thought of their dying.

And we go away, wishing we knew how to assure that it doesn't happen to our sons, to our children's children. We read our history, and we hope to study war no more, and we hold a little tighter to whatever it is we think we have.

There in the darkness, with the music celebrating the summer off in the distance, we remember and we hope.

Turning to go, though, looking at the row on row of names, we know there are few guarantees.

Hope, yes, but very, very few guarantees.

Reagan repeats Johnson's big mistake

Ronald Reagan seems to me to be moving ever closer to doing to conservatism in this country what Lyndon Johnson did to liberalism.

That is, I know, still not a popular interpretation of what has been happening for the past five years in this country, but I believe it deeply, and I worry about where we are heading.

Lyndon Johnson's mistake, you will remember, was his argument that we could afford both guns and butter, as he put it — the buildup in Vietnam and the expanding cost of the social programs launched as the Great Society — and that we could do it without paying for it as we went. He did not dare ask Congress or the country to pay the cost of sustaining the Vietnam War and at the same time supporting the effort to eradicate poverty in this country. The result was the unleashing of major, major inflationary pressures in the American economy.

Nov. 10, 1985

Whether you define yourself as a conservative or liberal, you have to try in some fundamental way to match resources to commitments.

Ronald Reagan came to office in 1981 believing that he could simultaneously reduce taxes, launch the largest military buildup in American peacetime history, and reshape American priorities by cutting deeply into social programs. He got ready concurrence in his tax cuts from an acquiescent Congress. Supposedly, any good conservative had to support this program. After all, among the tenets of American conservatism is supposed to be a belief that we must rely on the strength of our arms, that taxes are always higher than they ought to be, and that the government for at least the last 20 years and probably the last 50 has tried to do too much for us.

Because the Democrats were in such disarray and their political program so discredited, there wasn't much to stand in the way of this supposedly conservative Reagan revolution. There wasn't much to stand in the way of going "all the way with LBJ" after 1964, either.

Mr. Reagan, it seems to me, is in the 1980s running up against the same immutable truth that finally undid Mr. Johnson and undermined much of his domestic program: Whether you define yourself as a conservative or liberal, you have to try in some fundamental way to match resources to commitments. You have to offer something more than the airy promise that somehow the society will generate the means to pay for what you want to do.

This president, like Mr. Johnson before him, has sold a sufficient number of people on the notion that it doesn't matter. This president talks about cutting spending; but because he rules out so many areas of possible spending cuts and because there are such relatively limited savings to be made in those areas he defines as acceptable, nothing happens. Because he believes that any kind of tax increase is unconscionable — and in fact worse than doubling the national debt in five years and running up continuing $200-billion deficits — nothing happens.

Congress and the president have now finally begun to feel the pressure to appear to do something about the deficit. The president has all along embraced a lot of expedient alternatives to the simple and straightforward business of moving toward a balanced budget. "The devil in Congress made me do it," he says, and he embraces various bad schemes, such as the balanced-budget amendment to the Constitution and the line-item veto, to force him and Congress to do what they seem disinclined to do on their own.

The pressures have resulted in the bizarre dance routine now going on in Washington over the Gramm-Rudman bill. The Senate, acting without hearings, passed the bill. The House has been alternately trying to clean up and salvage the concept of some overall deficit-reduction plan or kill it by indirection. As it has dawned on the White House that the mechanism is going to force military spending cuts and ultimately a tax increase, the administration has begun to do some fancy stepping, too.

The truth is that a lot of people believe the country can and perhaps should continue to tolerate the big deficits. I believe they're wrong, and I believe the country is going to be badly hurt if we don't find some way to move in an orderly fashion toward better balance between the national government's income and outgo. We shouldn't bend the Constitution out of shape to do it, and we shouldn't compound our troubles with cures that make the economic malady worse.

There's nothing conservative about pretending the deficits don't matter. There's nothing conservative about offering unconstitutional expedients instead of solving the fundamental contradiction between the level at which we insist on spending and the level we have insisted on keeping our taxes.

In the long run, that will do little to conserve those values and achievements in this society that are well worth conserving. And Mr. Reagan, like Lyndon Johnson before him, will discover that the light at the end of the tunnel is a freight train coming at us.

Congress still deserves respect

Even if you dislike the speaker of the House, Jim Wright, you would have been hard-pressed not to be touched by the pathos of his farewell to the House of Representatives on Wednesday.

And if you really care about American institutions, you ought to spend some time worrying about how Congress should go about getting itself back on an even keel and restoring confidence in its institutional integrity.

I don't dislike Jim Wright or think of him as a true villain. I think of him as a man who, like many other public figures, found it easy to rationalize relationships and questionable actions rather than face them. I think of him as a proud, stubborn, smart but not always wise man who left himself vulnerable by not taking care about the appearance of things. I think of him as a man who was proud to be speaker, who loved the House, and who believed that he was being subjected to a new and draconian standard.

June 4, 1989

Speaker Wright is a tragedy. Congress is, overall and on balance, a success story.

In some ways that is true. Congress is not worse today than it has been in the past. It was Will Rogers, I think, who said that this country had the best Congress money could buy. Certainly, the role of special interests in the Congress of the late 19th Century was probably, if anything, even worse than anything we have been seeing lately.

Still, Congress is in deep trouble. That is so partly because Congress has been fuzzy about some of its standards. The lines it has attempted to draw — between honoraria and royalties, between campaign contributions and personal enrichment, between special interests and political action committees — are so indefensible as to invite the kind of reliance on technicalities through which Jim Wright sought to defend himself.

I've about had it with the cheap cynicism about our institutions. After Jim Wright finished his hour-long defense on Wednesday, a Detroit TV station's anchorperson came on with some flip comment about his "long-winded" statement. The man was, for crying out loud, delivering his valedictory. He was the first speaker in the history of the House to resign under such circumstances. Is that not worthy of a little more attention than a sound bite on the evening news?

Congress as an institution deserves to be held to a high standard, and Jim Wright certainly deserves to have to answer hard questions. But the institution, like the presidency, deserves some respect. We need to care about and to recognize the importance of the people's representatives. We can't afford simply to accept the cynical view of H.L. Mencken that the only way to look at a politician is down.

Public service is a high calling. I don't believe we should ever rejoice to see a Jim Wright or an Ed Meese or a Richard Nixon impaled on his sword. It doesn't make me happy to see a state legislator lamenting from his jail cell the fate that has befallen him. Congress is a splendid institution in many respects, and it is a tragedy when it — or the presidency, or the courts — is compromised.

Those who recognize that Congress is not a nuisance but a necessary instrument of our democracy need to step forward now to say that we must make important distinctions in the course of the current debate about ethics. I don't believe Jim Wright was pulled down by mindless cannibalism, but I do think we need some perspective on all this. Speaker Wright is a tragedy. Congress is, overall and on balance, a success story.

At the same time, those in Congress who truly love that body and who care about its reputation and theirs need to step forward and take charge now. They need to tidy up the rules and stop the leaks and set some standards and provide people with a reasonable assurance that the guilty will be punished and the innocent will not be tarred.

What has been happening is not a feeding frenzy. We have been seeing a feverish effort, in the absence of well-defined and well-understood standards, to challenge practices that should be challenged. What we need now is reform, not vengeance. What we need now are people who love this Republic and its institutions, and who want to save them from corruption within or contempt from outside.

Bush delivers high goals, weak leadership

As I watched George Bush deliver his State of the Union address last week, what struck me was how seldom I ever feel I dislike the man and how little I ever feel inspired or uplifted by him.

The speech itself seemed full of lofty aspirations for this country — goals that you might almost describe as liberal or progressive — and almost no ideas about how to carry them out. Do you want to see Americans better educated? So does George Bush. Do you worry about the two-income families and their frustration with trying to find trustworthy child care? So does Grandpa George. Do you fret about whether the deficit reduction is real and whether it is adequate? President Bush will see it through. Do you want clean air? So does Mr. Bush.

On virtually every issue that shows up as a big concern in the opinion polls, save abortion and China, George Bush was right there emoting over the need without taking any real responsibility. On education, for instance, he started off

FEB. 4, 1990

When Mr. Bush talked about the great events of 1989, the most incredible revolution of our times, I thought he was absolutely banal.

sounding the clarion call for the banishment of ignorance in this country — laying down very specific goals for American education — and then offered no real prescriptions, beyond his proposed investment in Head Start, about how to get there. It was as though John Kennedy had declared we would reach the moon by the end of the decade but left to goodwill and tokenism the question of how to get the job done.

And when Mr. Bush talked about the great events of 1989, the most incredible revolution of our times, I thought he was absolutely banal.

Mr. Bush obviously feels deeply the concern that so many have expressed about his ability to deal with what he, typically, calls "the vision thing." I thought in the foreign policy portion of his speech he was trying to say something equal to the occasion. What bothers me is that he manages to make it seem like the report from the membership chairman at the Amarillo Rotary Club. These are extraordinary events, laden with peril as well as promise. It isn't enough just to call them great events. The country and the world need some sense of how the American president thinks we can capitalize on this moment in history.

A few weeks ago, just before the Panamanian invasion and just after a visit to the White House, I wrote of George Bush's innate caution. Within days of that column, almost within hours, he had ordered the troops into Panama. It was hardly a cautious or timid act. "Caution" was probably a poor choice of words on my part. Still, though, there seems to be a timidity about the power of ideas and ideals and an inability really to project this country's leadership and to bring its weight down on the right side of issues around the world.

This country does not require that its leaders be great orators. We've only had a couple of truly masterful ones in the White House since Franklin Roosevelt: John Kennedy and Ronald Reagan. Lyndon Johnson managed to rise to the occasion a couple of times during the civil rights revolution — his "We shall overcome" speech made me weep for joy — but he became progressively more banal. Richard Nixon has become a fine speaker as he has aged, but he seldom has inspired. Gerald Ford exuded sincerity but offered little that was memorable. And Jimmy Carter only rarely managed even to put the accent on the right syllable. Dwight Eisenhower was a terrible extemporaneous speaker, but there were set-piece occasions — his farewell address comes to mind — when he managed to say something important and profound. Harry Truman could say it straight, but he was a better thinker and leader than an orator.

Mr. Bush can overcome his inability to deal with "the vision thing," at least politically. Who can argue with 81-percent approval ratings? The country obviously feels pretty good about the state of the world and consequently pretty good about him.

Nonetheless, there come moments when you badly need a president who can stand up and offer a speech that is both substance and style. You need not merely to like the leader personally, but to get some real sense of where he wants to take us and how he expects to do it. Maybe no new taxes and troop cuts in Europe will suffice. Certainly that's a ready-made political combination. At some point, though, you need to project something more, to offer speeches that combine style and substance to mobilize the country for challenges that plainly lie in front of us. And that, despite the opinion polls, President Bush is still struggling to learn how to do.

He is comfortable; he is conventional and probably competent in his approach to management. But is he really much of a leader? I think that question will become more urgent whenever the Ship of State slips, as inevitably it will, into somewhat rougher waters.

U.S. must heed its own lessons on poverty

"The Grapes of Wrath" may seem an oddly dated play for the 1990s, and Salt Lake City may seem an odd place to see the dramatization of John Steinbeck's account of a Depression-era family heading for California with the whole family packed into an old truck.

But I found the play, which I saw at the Pioneer Theater on the University of Utah campus last weekend, to be haunting and painfully relevant to the issue of what is happening to the poor in the America of the 1990s. That feeling was reinforced by an exhibit of photographic portraits of the homeless of Salt Lake City in the galleries adjacent to the theater. I was also struck by how often one encounters panhandlers even in Salt Lake City, on streets almost in the shadow of the Mormon Tabernacle.

Oct. 6, 1991

There isn't much constituency for compassion these days, and there isn't much appetite for hearing about the darker side of America's situation today.

For many of us, of course, the story of people driven off the land in Oklahoma and Arkansas, going to California looking for work, seems long ago and far away. Many Americans have indeed prospered during the 1980s and 1990s, including many whose parents or grandparents made similar treks in search of opportunity in the hard-knock times of the Great Depression. There are many voices who argue, as Ronald Reagan did, that the rising tide will lift all boats and that the marketplace alone will suffice to create opportunity for all.

To the Joads of John Steinbeck's story, the Depression meant being cut loose from the land that had sustained them, pushed off as landowners themselves tried to survive through mechanization. And so they went off to California (or in the case of a lot of other people, to "Dee-troit") on the strength of a rumor and a handbill full of promise of work. They were scorned and harassed as Arkies and Okies if they were white or greeted with even more hostility if they were black.

In the Great Depression, poverty was, of course, far more widespread than it is now. In these days, those who can hustle can often find work. But there remain pockets here — big pockets, many of them in our cities, some in isolated rural areas — that have lost their economic function. In every city — and especially in cities such as Detroit, with an old industrial base so badly eroded — you can scarcely walk down the street without encountering on every block the evidence of people left behind by the prosperity of the '80s. Few cities are insulated from the evidence that there are, indeed, still two Americas.

In some ways, this is or ought to be the best of times. Communism has collapsed, and such ideas as democracy and human rights and market economics have demonstrated around the world the power of their appeal. This country's long and determined stand against the tyranny represented by the Soviet Union has paid off. Containment worked. And there are many, many aspects of life in this blessed Republic that are the standard to which the rest of the world aspires. There is much to celebrate in America.

There are some dangers, though, that worry me and that particularly seem troublesome against the backdrop of the reminders of the Great Depression and the realities of the homeless and the poor in the America of the 1990s. This country and indeed capitalism itself faced a crisis in the 1930s. The threat of communism was real because there were a lot of desperate people ready to try any kind of change. What happened, though, was that America's capitalist system, far from being destroyed, was tempered with compassion. We softened the harsh edges of our system and thereby, as I read history, helped to save the American system.

What scares me today is the possibility that too many people will be bedazzled by the great events unfolding in the world beyond our borders, and so forgetful of how important it was that we tried to humanize the American system, that we will slip into a crisis of our own. Can we really tolerate the levels of violence, the gap between those of us who have prospered and those who haven't? Can we simply deal with racism in America through benign neglect? Can we ignore the desperate condition of the cities? And is there anything other than either some old socialist canards or some neo-Darwinist harshness that can help us to overcome the nightmares in the American dream?

There isn't much constituency for compassion these days, and there isn't much appetite for hearing about the darker side of America's situation today. Still, I have to say it. There are a lot of people who have been hurt, as well as many who have been helped, by what happened in the '80s. When I hear people denouncing as "socialism" even efforts to have the state equalize school funding in Michigan, I wonder how far we have gone toward foreclosing opportunity for those who have been left behind by the prosperity of the '80s. Isn't there a danger here that we are forgetting at least some of the lessons of our history? I see a real threat.

THE WORLD

From Anwar Sadat to Saddam Hussein

Sadat renews fragile hope of peace

On this Sunday morning in Detroit, most of us will be caught up in the drama and historic importance of President Anwar Sadat's journey to Jerusalem.

With the advent of television and the effect it has in bringing to life distant events, we are as much a part of this trip from Cairo to Jerusalem as we are of what happened in Ann Arbor yesterday, what friends and neighbors might say when we meet them, what happens in the state Capitol or downtown.

Besides, this is such a transcendental event — a symbolic, albeit still tentative, break with the frustrating patterns of the past — that it is very real and alive and a part of our lives.

Yet we do not need to be reminded of the dangers that President Sadat has exposed himself to as a result of his grand initiative. Bold deeds are spurned by timid men because they have risks. The risks are real. Consider what has followed in the wake of Sadat's initiative: a cabinet crisis, outspoken criticism in the Arab world, the bombing of the Egyptian Embassy in Damascus.

Nov. 20, 1977

There are times when only an act of personal courage can have any chance of changing the course of history. This may be one of those times.

Yet there are times when only an act of personal courage can have any chance of changing the course of history. This may be one of those times. There has been a moment of opportunity in the Middle East — the chance to reconcile the irreconcilable — and it seemed possibly to be slipping away.

That opportunity was the result partly of the long-standing, patient U.S.

effort to build bridges, starting even before the Kissinger era at the State Department and continuing through the period of shuttle diplomacy up through the Carter administration. And the result has been to create a climate in which peace seemed barely possible because the alternatives were so unthinkable.

When President Jimmy Carter talked with members of our editorial board in Detroit recently, he said he thinks the chance for peace is real now: that all the parties realize how essential it is, that they know they must compromise and change. The present situation provides only the security of armed stalemate.

I have believed that security for all can be consistent with the idea of accommodation by all: that somehow the Palestinian question can be reconciled with Israel's right to exist and to be secure.

Now President Sadat has opened a door on that possibility. Not that the Israelis can achieve a peace for themselves simply by making peace with Sadat. There is a danger in pushing the bilateral discussions too far. It is not merely the danger that the problems between the Israelis and the Jordanians, and the Israelis and the Syrians, or the problems of the Palestinians, will be left to fester.

The greater danger may be not that Israel will be isolated but that Egypt will: that Sadat will be pulled down by the passionate divisions within the Arab world, that we will be left with nothing but the personal courage of a single leader and the rejection of his symbolic act by his own people.

So while the burden is heavy on President Sadat this weekend, it is also heavy on Menachem Begin and the Israeli government. A grand initiative calls for a response; a failure to show movement may well destroy Sadat and the hope for peace that he has opened up.

In all this, it is important for us in this country to be patient with the zigs and zags on the road to peace. Many of the president's efforts have been misunderstood and maligned. A lot of people have chased after a lot of shadows, partly out of the knowledge that one day, out of the shadows, some new and fundamentally different reality might emerge.

With Sadat's journey to Jerusalem, that new and fundamentally different reality may be beginning to emerge from the shadows. Is it to be a vision of a peace for the Middle East, or is it a harsh reality that will dash all our hopes and leave us once again with the thought that men cry peace, and there is no peace?

This day, beginning as it does the week of the American Thanksgiving festival, is a time for hope and for thankfulness that this moment of symbolic opportunity has come.

In the quiet of this Sunday, we should also understand what is at stake and how much the hopes of mankind are riding on the process that Anwar Sadat has now set in motion.

The journey to Jerusalem will not mean peace in itself. It should be only a way station on the road to Geneva. After this weekend, though, we may begin to sense the opportunity that is at hand and to know whether peace is achievable.

In America, and around the world, it is a time for quiet reflection, for hope and for prayer.

The true drama of the Polish workers

The workers of Poland.

I can't quit thinking about the workers of Poland.

I keep thinking about the risks they and their country have incurred, and the odds against their succeeding at changing the communist system under which they must operate.

I think, too, of the tragic history of Poland, so often trampled by the armies of Europe, so nationalistic, so rich in music and culture, so deeply Catholic, so fervent in its yearning for independence.

I remember how my heart leapt, earlier, as I thought of the patriots in Hungary and Czechoslovakia, and of the bedraggled warriors of Afghanistan, and I know that I dare not let myself hope too much for the people of Poland. They risk much, and they always gain small victories, and always there is the long shadow of the Soviet Union.

The church in Poland has come under criticism, both within Poland and without, for its failure to support more forthrightly the workers and their push for independence. Yet it seems to me that Poland is a place where the church, over an

SEPT. 14, 1980

Poland's worker strikes are dramatic evidence that those who believe there is an inexorable Red tide in the world, that the Soviet Union is inevitably on the move and the United States on the decline, are not necessarily right.

extended period of time, has played a remarkable and important role in keeping alive both the concept and the partial reality of independence. It has long played a careful game there, always living on the edge.

Yet who can doubt that Poland is different from much of the rest of the Warsaw bloc, that it has more perfectly nurtured its religious traditions and its nationalistic yearnings, that its spirit is more resistant to the oppressive presence of the Soviet behemoth?

Poland is important in another way. Its worker strikes are dramatic evidence that those who believe there is an inexorable Red tide in the world, that the Soviet Union is inevitably on the move and the United States on the decline, are not necessarily right. When I look at the world, I do not see the inevitable decline of the West, and I do not see a newly ascendant Soviet Union.

I see a mixed pattern. I see the United States using former Soviet bases in Somalia; I see the profundity of the Chinese-Soviet split; I see the chance at least in Zimbabwe and much of the rest of southern Africa of heading off a race war that would make that area a Cold War cockpit. I see a strategic balance that is more favorable to the United States than current political debate might suggest. I see signs of failure and weakness and uncertainty in the Soviet Union. I even see signs that the world reaction to the Soviet invasion of Afghanistan, while ineffectual at stopping the invasion, has given the Soviet Union a bit more reticence about heavy-handed intrusion into Eastern Europe.

The contrary picture — the weakening of the Western alliance, the trouble we have had in maintaining the efficiency of the all-volunteer army, the instability of the Middle East, the Soviet Union's success in fishing in the troubled waters of northern Africa — is real, too. And there is always the possibility that a weak or unstable Soviet Union might be more dangerous than a strong, confident Soviet Union. Paranoia and vulnerability may be more dangerous than strength.

The point is, though, that the world is always more complicated than the stereotyped Cold War view. The struggle for freedom takes many forms, occurs almost without regard to ideology. Yesterday Poland, today Turkey, tomorrow Peru. It is odd how we absentmindedly accept the Marxist view of the world, that what is really going on is a war between systems, that the real threat to the West is a system, a conspiracy, a bloc.

In the real world, it seems to me, the struggle, whether within the Soviet bloc or in Western societies or in the Third World, is over how we find the balance between the individual and the state, how we preserve latitude for the worker and the individual while maintaining efficiency and order and productivity in the larger society. Marx is mocked when the workers mount the barricades in a supposedly classless state, a workers' paradise. We are mocked when we lose sight of the central role of the individual in the American ideal.

It is hard not to get caught up in a thoroughly romantic view of the Polish workers' strike, to forget the harsh economic and energy realties that have been forcing hard choices on both communist and noncommunist societies.

The struggle is real. The issues are real and earnest. The risks are everpresent. The courage is magnificent. We wish we could do more to make a difference. The question is whether we can know the difference between drama and melodrama. Drama is more complex, more subtle.

In the end, though, it is more moving, more satisfying, more important. It may be more tragic, too. But that is what makes the drama, ultimately, more heroic and significant. And that is what makes the story of what has been happening these last few weeks in Poland matter so much.

The Iron Curtain falls hard on ideas

Irkutsk — Long before we sat down with a group of academicians in this Siberian city, we had had a pretty good foretaste of how the Soviet system responds to alien ideas.

At customs in Leningrad's international airport, you could see what made them uneasy. Recent issues of Time and Newsweek, filled as they were with the accounts of the destruction of KAL 007, were seized. A cartoon parody of Lenin was obviously a threat. And a Defense Department handout — an assessment of Soviet military strength — was certain to raise questions, and did.

If I may jump ahead of myself for a moment, the same pattern prevailed as we were going through Soviet customs on the way out of the country. They were, again, frightened of ideas and information: the handouts we had been given by our embassy and their news agencies; a diary a Soviet citizen had pressed on us on the Trans-Siberian Railway, an enigmatic book filled with hand-sketched illustrations about freedom and American rock music; my wife's address book, which they scanned page by page. The customs agents seemed to be working from a list of passport numbers; the only common denominator seemed to be whether you had made any effort to get beyond Intourist's prepackaged contacts. They seized nothing, but it was striking to see how much the focus was on books, ideas, information.

Our session here in this easternmost city on our tour included a broad range

OCT. 21, 1983

It's odd what the customs people worry about. Not fur hats or currency or souvenirs, really. Just ideas. Ideas coming in and ideas going out.

of intellectuals, including a poet, a publisher, a novelist, the head of the local writers' union, the head of the local artists' union, the local representatives of Novosti and TASS, a sprinkling of professors.

For a while, the discussion centered on such issues as women in arts and letters (there were none in their group), what they read about America (they complained about the expense of American publications), and the differences in sex education and sexual explicitness in fiction. On the latter subject, there was so much guffawing that in playing my tape of the session, I could barely hear the speakers. They are, they said, less explicit than Americans, but that does not mean Russians are cold people.

Then, the question turned, as any such conversation must, to the banning of books and the exiling of writers. What about Solzhenitsyn? Pasternak? Had they had the chance to read or to see "Dr. Zhivago"? They had, but they thought it pretty irrelevant in some of its detail. Such as? Well, the taking of Lara's temperature was not done in the Russian way. She didn't look Russian. Were they able to see current American movies and publications? Yes, some.

The heart of the discussion for us was what turned into a frank defense of the right of the state to stop publication of a book if banning it served the good of the state, or if the publication violated Leninist principles.

In a discussion with the director of the big library at Novosibirsk — eight million volumes, one of the more important collections in the Soviet Union — the subject came up again. Could a Soviet citizen find in his library the kinds of publications taken from us at the Leningrad airport? American publications cost a lot, he said, and some technical journals have been denied him at any price. Were there books by Sakharov in his library? His own background was that of a mathematician, he said, and he did not know.

Then, one of our group asked the director if he had read the statement in the little pamphlet we had been handed on his library. "The chief task of libraries," it said, "is to actively promote the policy of the Communist Party and the Soviet government ... " Do you, as a librarian, subscribe to that? Yes, said Mr. Boris Stepanovich Yelepov of the State Public Library of Scientific and Technical Materials. At that point, there seemed not much else to discuss about the breadth or limits of his library. He had defined it for us.

Later, in Moscow with a sophisticated group of Soviet journalists, I had to challenge the intellectual constraints again. "One of our revolutionaries, Thomas Jefferson, argued that only through recurrent revolutions can a revolution be kept pure," I said. "I hear a lot here about what is revolutionary and what is counterrevolutionary. My question is, who decides which is which?"

The response, as always, was that there is criticism, there are controversies, there are intellectual debates. It wasn't very persuasive. The Helsinki basket of information and ideas from outside is extraordinarily empty in the Soviet Union. And when you hear the argument from otherwise intelligent men and women, who plainly know in their hearts how convoluted their defense of suppression of information is, it is doubly sad. It's odd what the customs people worry about. Not fur hats or currency or souvenirs, really. Just ideas. Ideas coming in and ideas going out. Books. Whatever offends the state.

They worry about the sort of stuff that revolutions used to be made of.

Forces of pain tighten in South Africa

"Living in South Africa," said the Cape Town editor, "is like living with a toothache. Sometimes, when I wake up on a beautiful morning, I can convince myself that somehow it will all work out. But the toothache is always there."

As I read this past week of the new restrictions on political opposition in South Africa, I thought of him and his book-lined home and his gracious wife and his talkative 11-year-old daughter.

I thought, too, of the misty evening when I had gone by myself to stand along the promenade just below my hotel in Cape Town. I alternately stood and sat in the damp chill, looking back at the brilliantly white houses and flats, occasionally feeling the spray of the crashing surf, marveling at the beauty and solitude of that moment. I needed the time to try to absorb the enormity of what I had been seeing in South Africa.

There had been so many impressions: the wretchedly crowded and isolated townships, with the shanties and the palpable anger; the evening over good South African wine with mostly reformist professor types; the chance encounter in

FEB. 28, 1988

South Africa is not, of course, merely a monstrous evil. It is also a monstrous tragedy — people caught in a grinding process that they cannot control, forces propelling people headlong toward disaster.

a United Democratic Front office with a young black man whose father had disappeared into the prison system and died; the conversations with parents, black and white, worried about the future their children might face in South Africa; the picture-postcard street scenes on a Sunday afternoon in Pretoria. The beauty of the country is truly haunting, the pain deep and manifested in a multitude of ways.

That was May of 1986. Today, that sad and beautiful land seems to be sinking ever deeper into the abyss of repression and hopelessness. This week, the government announced the banning of 17 different antiapartheid organizations, barred the big labor federation from political activities, and started a campaign to isolate and silence the most troublesome individual activists. It is an unmistakable signal that the government is giving up on its former strategy of trying, by means of modest reforms, to co-opt some elements of its black majority. There is no longer even the pretense of reform or accommodation.

Two years ago, South Africa often seemed an oddly contradictory place. Repression existed side by side with a curious compulsion to cloak everything in the mask of due process. The control of the Nationalist Party was secure, but one did not have to search hard to find critics willing to talk openly about apartheid. Lawlessness seemed to exist side by side with an almost fastidious obsession with the forms of democracy.

Yet I found South Africa to be a place where I felt myself in the presence of a monstrous evil. Life is full of contradictions, of course, and it should not surprise us that evil people sometimes nurture flowers, that they care about the form and the trappings that put a good face on the evil in which they are entrapped. Somehow it always does surprise us, though. It looks so beautiful.

South Africa is not, of course, merely a monstrous evil. It is also a monstrous tragedy — people caught in a grinding process that they cannot control, forces propelling people headlong toward disaster. Many of them are good people; some of them even behave with courage and decency and a sense of outrage at the status quo. They lack the power to change the prevailing order. They are caught between the reality of repression and the possibility of eventual revolution.

As the tragedy deepens in South Africa, the pain will deepen, too. The choices for people will become harder. How much do you compromise with the underlying reality of the repressive state? What do you expect of or fear from revolution? Is there any kind of happy future along the shore in Cape Town? Is there any balm in Gilead?

In the mist of a May evening, I grieved for the people of South Africa who have kept hoping for some basis for change, change for the better, change that might promise peace.

After last week, I grieve even more.

It is hard to see how and when the pain will ever end.

It must be hard on even a beautiful morning or a misty evening.

From China, a lesson on freedom and flags

As Independence Day approaches, this country is in danger of drowning in a sea of demagoguery and missing the real point about the values for which the Republic stands.

On two subjects — the suppression of the pro-democracy student protests in Beijing and the Supreme Court's decision that flag burning is a protected form of protest — the politicians are really muddying the waters. The sentiments that have made both such volatile political issues are understandable, but the distinctions about what makes this country great keep getting lost in the turmoil.

On China, the politicians sense that the American public is so moved by the student protests and so impatient with President George Bush's response that Congress just has to do something. I'm impatient with the president's response, but I also think we have to find an appropriate way to channel our anger. And we ought to remember how often sanctions have backfired on us in the past. There is a need for selectivity. There is also a need for the American people to express very clearly what our values are and how much we identify with the now-suppressed protests in China. So we need to keep searching for ways to make our voices heard.

JULY 2, 1989

The most powerful, unstoppable force in the world is the contagion of human freedom.

Meanwhile, the Supreme Court's decision that the Constitution protects free speech, including the right to burn even a beloved symbol of the Republic such as the flag, has set off a wave of pre-Independence Day rhetoric and showmanship such as we haven't seen in many a year.

Some of the same people who protested so vehemently against the suppression of the protests in China have gone crazy over the Supreme Court's protection of even unpopular protest in the United States. Yet isn't the Supreme Court trying to say precisely that what sets us apart from countries such as China is not merely the color of our flag, but the content of our Constitution and our democratic values? Do we love the flag more than freedom?

Don't distort what I'm saying. I do not like to see anyone desecrate the flag. I've spent an inordinate number of years trying to teach small children that you don't let the flag touch the ground, that you treat it with respect, that you don't either burn the flag or wrap yourself in it under my value system.

What I'm trying to say is that if we really want to exercise our patriotism this Independence Day, should we not proclaim values even more than we wave flags? Do we wish the Chinese would respect our flag or our values? There isn't much chance that they will go very far with the former. There is, in the long run, a lot of chance that people around the world will not only respect but actually embrace the democratic ideals that are the foundation of this Republic.

If we have learned anything over the last decade or so, it is that the ideals of democracy and human rights have proved themselves to be incredibly powerful instruments of foreign policy. People do yearn to breathe free, from the gulag of the Soviet Union, to the streets of Beijing, to the long-repressed precincts of Chile, to the steaming fields of Nicaragua and El Salvador, to the blood-stained jungles of the Philippines. They are weary of the totalitarians of the Left and of the Right. In many, many places, people are ready to fight and to die for the right to speak their mind and demand their rights.

The most powerful, unstoppable force in the world is the contagion of human freedom. We're talking about the power of ideas and ideals. The most amazing truth of all about the power of these ideas and ideals is how unable governments have been to seal out the subversion of freedom. Was it the American government that ignited the protests in Tiananmen Square? Hardly. Was it the power of ideas and ideals? You bet. The ideas and ideals have been spread insidiously, from people to people.

Does that not suggest some possibility, then, that we as ordinary people can express our solidarity with the people of China in a far more direct, less complicated way than our government can? I think maybe it does. If the China question is too complicated for governments, why not personal expressions of support and rage?

We can waste a lot of breath and confuse a lot of issues this Fourth of July if we spend our time yelling about this mostly imaginary threat to our flag. Or we can try to celebrate our freedom by proclaiming its relevance for the people of China and other places where people want to be free.

Why not start a people-to-people movement — letters of protests, speeches of encouragement, messages of solidarity — that speaks to our brothers and sisters in China and elsewhere? Yes, we love our flag. But we love freedom more. We love our freedom, and we intend to celebrate it. We believe it is relevant to you. We abhor the price your government is exacting from you over the very same values so protected by our Constitution. We may not know just how to stop your government from trampling your rights. Nonetheless, we want you to know where we stand.

When the U.S. sides with oppressors

As we were boarding the train to Budapest, saying good-bye, my wife tried discreetly to thrust some American dollars into the jacket pocket of her Czech cousin.

"No, Kathy," he said. "We have enough to buy what we need ..." He handed the money back.

And then, as we prepared to go, he said, sadly but matter-of-factly, "But we are not free."

Those words have been ringing in my ears since that trip in 1982. The Cold War took on a whole new meaning. Stalinism became not just a concept in a history book.

In the years since, I have been to a lot of other places where, when people say, "We are not free," you know it isn't simply rhetoric. I was in the Soviet Union in 1983 and heard and saw echoes of those words. I heard the echoes in Cuba and, despite what all the apologists say, to some degree in Nicaragua.

I also heard them in South Africa and

Nov. 19, 1989

It is one thing to rejoice at the near collapse of the communist economic system and the Stalinist methods of control in Eastern Europe. It is quite another to conclude that those are the only kinds of tyranny in the world.

El Salvador and Chile. "But we are not free." The tyrannies take many forms: the tyranny of the Left, the tyranny of the oligarchy, the tyranny of Pinochet, the tyranny of the death squads, the tyranny of blind and stupid and overbearing U.S. presence.

As we watch the incredible pace of change in Eastern Europe, with "democratization" and "liberalization" the watchwords, we in the West and particularly the United States had better be careful of our blind spots. It is one thing to rejoice at the near collapse of the communist economic system and the Stalinist methods of control in Eastern Europe. It is quite another to conclude that those are the only kinds of tyranny in the world.

Nowhere is that insight more important than in Latin America and particularly Central America. I happen to think that U.S. policy has generally been wretched toward Latin America and particularly Central America. Again and again, over years and years, we have not only intervened but intervened in the clumsiest and most counterproductive ways. Do we wonder that we, the United States, often seem a more likely source of danger than the Soviet Union?

Even if we don't think much of the Sandinista revolution — and I do think it is a perverted revolution in important respects — what sense can we make of the contras policy? Even if we abhor the Noriega regime in Panama, can we really feel comfortable with the gang-that-couldn't-shoot-straight interventionism that has passed for American policy over the past few years?

The postwar generation, thanks largely to the leadership of Harry S Truman, fashioned a policy that succeeded. Containment worked. The United States was strong against the Soviet Union, but for the most part not reckless. It was powerful and steady in its commitment to resistance to the Soviet Union's expansion; it was willing to let time work its magic. Time did work its magic. The democratic ideals and free-market bias of the West have become the stronger force in the world. The internal contradictions of Marxism have proved more contradictory than the modified capitalism of the West. Why? Because the West learned that, yes, political freedom and economic decentralization are powerful engines for progress, and that, yes, we can ameliorate the built-in weaknesses of the capitalist system.

What concerns me, though, is that we may misread what has happened and not deal with the flaws in our own democracy. Is oligarchy the only alternative to revolution in Central America? Is violent, crypto-Marxist revolution the only answer to a repressive elite in a place such as El Salvador? The attempt in the early Reagan years to rationalize our tyrants, while decrying repression by their tyrants, seemed to me to be a terrible mistake.

We can't compartmentalize freedom that way. If democratization is important to a miner in the Soviet Union, why isn't it important to a coffee worker in El Salvador? If we don't like what the Soviet troops did to Afghanistan, can we shed a tear for what American troops sometimes did to corrupt and distort Honduras?

And it seems terribly important to have a president of the United States do a better job of articulating why freedom is indivisible, and why our ideals matter in our sphere of influence, and why you can protect American security without perverting American ideals.

It seems terribly important, but I don't see it happening.

There are still too many places in the world where the cry is still "we are not free."

And there are still too many places in the world where it is not clear whether the United States has figured out how to side with the oppressed rather than the oppressors.

Victory offers lesson on failed policy

Along about the first of March, I begin to fear, we may well see a headline on the Detroit News editorial page that says, "Invade Nicaragua."

And we may begin to hear that troops are being airlifted to Honduras, on the premise that the February election in Nicaragua, having been "stolen" by the Sandinistas, shows the need for direct U.S. action to liberate Nicaragua.

That fantasy may seem farfetched, but the euphoria over the success of the invasion of Panama and the Bush administration's impatience with questions about legal process certainly combine to give me pause. In an insomniac interlude after midnight on Friday morning, I watched with amazement a CNN tape of the U.S. State Department briefing on the surrender of Manuel Noriega. What really stunned me was the absence of any pretense of concern for Panamanian sovereignty. The whole concept was that the United States was in de facto control of Panama and Gen. Noriega knew he had to deal with the United States.

JAN. 7, 1990

If war is really the extension of diplomacy, it is also usually at least partly a result of the failure of diplomacy.

The Bush administration clearly sees an opportunity to assert U.S. power in a very blunt and direct way to clean up what are seen as long-standing nuisances in this hemisphere. The people of Panama also very clearly welcome liberation from the tender mercies of the Noriega crowd. The rationale for direct action in Panama was pretty strong, given all this country had done to create the monster in the first place. And this invasion met the Machiavelli test: It was done with enough swiftness and force that it worked. The same George

Bush who has seemed so cautious about embracing the aspirations of Chinese students or the captive nations of the Baltic moved decisively and almost exultantly to use force in Panama.

Yet the very moment of euphoria about the use of force is also a time when you ought to ask the hard questions. I remember reading how, at the first battle of Manassas, or Bull Run, the crowds from Washington went out with their picnic baskets to watch what was expected to be a rout, only to scramble back to safety when the battle proved a little less simple. The rush to glory, however justified by real grievances, often has other implications less instantly clear.

If war is really the extension of diplomacy, it is also usually at least partly a result of the failure of diplomacy. The use of force may be ultimately the only answer in some situations, but that usually reflects the failure of policy in the months and years that precede the resort to force. And U.S. policy in Central America, often wrong and counterproductive through the years, is not transformed into a success in a few days' work by the 82nd Airborne.

I think there is a strong case now for an assertive, even aggressive U.S. policy in Latin America, but a very different policy than that now being pursued. I want to see the Soviet Union abandon its monstrous subsidy of the neo-Stalinist, unreconstructed regime of Fidel Castro. I don't share the enthusiasm of some of our friends on the Left who keep trying to rationalize the Sandinistas in Nicaragua any more than I can swallow what the apologists for the government in El Salvador put forward. I do believe the United States has some security interests in this hemisphere; and although those interests don't justify invasions, they do warrant concern and strong action.

Look beyond the euphoria of this moment, though, and think about how we go about promoting change. Ronald Reagan's strong defense stand in the '80s undoubtedly had a role in the liberation of Eastern Europe, but the real success story is to be found in 45 years of steady, restrained, pragmatic pursuit of the policy of containment by American presidents and Western allies, and in the heroic people of Eastern Europe who refused to sell their souls to their communist overlords.

With the pressure now inside the Soviet Union's self-proclaimed borders, we are entering a dangerous period. The temptation to unleash the Red Army will be strong. George Bush's insistence on seeing this as largely a question of power — what advantage can we take of the present weakness of the Soviet Union? — could come back to haunt us. We ought not always to rule out the use of U.S. power. Indeed, the cheers in Panama City suggest that there was a strong element of "just cause" in this intervention. The resort to force, though, is a game others can play.

So let us be a little thoughtful about our infatuation with the U.S. role of policeman of the hemisphere, if not of the world. If we are shrewder about our diplomacy and about what the real threats to us are, maybe we can avoid having to confess that our diplomacy has failed and that we have to resort to force to shape the world to our tastes.

And maybe we can enter this brave new world more confident that our country is determined to be right as well as strong.

As world changes, values need rethinking

Czechoslovakia's communists, says that country's ambassador to the United States, Rita Klimova, have disappeared like "steam over a pot."

And with the old order vanishing in Eastern Europe — with what seemed unthinkable suddenly the daily reality — the Czechs are struggling like everyone else in Europe to redefine themselves.

During a seminar this past week at Northwestern University, I listened to a succession of people from Eastern Europe struggling to define the new order that is emerging and the problems that lie on the way to the creation of the new order. What impressed me most was how much they talked of the need to discover a new moral basis for their societies.

The challenge varies from country to country. Poland, perhaps the most thoroughly Catholic country in the world, is returning to its Catholic, moralist roots. Krzystof Sliwinski, a senior editor at Gazeta Wyborcza, talked of the crucial role that Pope John Paul II had played in ending the isolation of Poland, beginning with his 1979 visit to Poland. John Paul, said Mr. Sliwinski, helped Poland to preserve its deeply rooted Catholic, moralist values "during those hardest years of our history."

MARCH 25, 1990

This is a period of great opportunity and great danger in the world. As Martin Palous said, new governments face a serious question of "what to do with all that celebration."

When historians write the record of this era, I suspect they are going to have to pay special attention to the role of the pope in defining a non-Marxist, pro-democratic alternative not just in Eastern Europe, but in Latin America and elsewhere. I am not Catholic myself and am uncomfortable with much of what I see as the authoritarianism and paternalism of the Catholic Church. But I do believe you have to credit the pope with articulating a passion for justice and the poor and at the same time for saying bluntly what a monstrous fraud Marxism has represented.

During many of the years of the Cold War, I have been troubled by the limitations of anticommunism in and of itself as a unifying theme for American foreign policy and for dealing with the world generally. We tended to let ourselves be defined and even be manipulated by what we were against. If Chile's Augusto Pinochet was against communism, he must somehow be a friend of ours. If something served to halt the spread of communism, it was supposed to be, almost automatically, something good.

Anticommunism sometimes seemed to free us from the need for thinking. To those forced to live under the authoritarian governments of the Warsaw bloc, there was a similar escape from responsibility. As Martin Palous, a foreign policy adviser to Czech President Vaclav Havel, told the seminar: "Totalitarianism is a system where no one is responsible for anything."

But the events of the '80s have forced many of us, in many parts of the world, to try to rethink what our values are. What does democracy mean? What is the moral base for our societies? What is justice? What is freedom? The creation of this new world is forcing a stunning rejection of the Cold War framework into which we have been locked for so many of the years since World War II.

This is a period of great opportunity and great danger in the world. As Mr. Palous said, the new governments face a serious question of "what to do with all that celebration." The great fear that I heard expressed is not of reaction — not the restoration of the communist oligarchy — but the possibility of what Mr. Sliwinski characterized as a South America-style populism, the potential for a demagogue in the Juan Peron tradition.

This debate over the moral foundations of the newly emerging democracies in Eastern Europe may seem esoteric, but it is important. It is really very hard to find the words to capture the significance of this moment in the history of the world, and particularly of Europe. We are dealing with what Mr. Palous called the "very spectacular disintegration of totalitarianism."

The United States has been in many ways a bystander, and sometimes almost a befuddled bystander, as this drama unfolds. Although many of the values — democracy, the concept of the individual's worth, the idea of the consent of the government, the emphasis on due process — are derived from our own revolution, we sometimes seem less passionately engaged about them than do the patriots of Eastern Europe. And though an emphasis on the role of the market economy is revolutionizing economies in places as different as Sao Paulo and Warsaw, we in the United States seem sometimes more caught up in the gaudy trimmings of consumerism than in finding ways to be more productive.

I think we ought to be doing some fresh thinking about what all this means for us and our country. How can we get beyond the stale liberal/conservative arguments to build a competent society that fosters and rewards initiative and yet deals humanely with those who need special help? How can we educate people better instead of merely paying more for education? How can we place fresh demands on our politicians for competence and a concern for right and wrong?

So let us focus, as we must, on the rise of a new and more powerful Germany. Let us think about why the Soviet Union is in an advanced stage of deterioration, and let us wrestle with the question of what it means.

But let us somehow find time, too, to think about what in our Judeo-Christian tradition can speak to this moment and to the rest of our lives. The last few years have destroyed many of the assumptions that have governed our lives in the 20th Century. Maybe, like the East Europeans, what we need to do is to try harder than ever to find what is good and distinctive and right about our traditions. Maybe if we do that thoughtfully enough, we will discover a moral basis for our society, too.

With Iraq, it was not wrong to go to war

To many of those whose worldview was shaped by the Vietnam era, the U.S. decision to use force against Iraq is a stunning throwback to the *pax Americana* days of Lyndon Johnson.

They see George Bush as striding across the world stage, trying to prove he is not a wimp by unleashing the instruments of death and war, ignoring chances for peace and negotiation in his lust for war. And seeing the editorial page of the Detroit Free Press supporting, albeit reluctantly, the authorization for the president to use force in the Persian Gulf, some of them fear that we are caught up in a betrayal of basic principle and a proud history.

Those reactions are understandable but painful to me. War is always a lousy option, even when you think other options have been exhausted. Yes, I think we could have avoided this war if only we could go back and repeal the history of 19th- and 20th-Century colonialism, if only U.S. policy itself had not made so many wrong turns. Yes, I do wish my government had paid more attention to making itself less vulnerable to oil shocks and had played a less dangerous game with arms and oil in the Middle East. And no, I don't believe the United States can be policeman to the world or that anyone should die simply to protect our inalienable right to drive 90 m.p.h.

But I did believe and I do believe that the United States was right, and the

JAN. 20, 1991

This is not Vietnam, and it is not World War III. It is a situation where an international coalition can reasonably hope to act together to check the ambitions of a dangerous man and a mistaken nation.

international community was right, to confront Saddam Hussein's aggression. As much as I think we ought to have a bias against war, I cannot ultimately come to a pacifist position. This is not Vietnam, and it is not World War III. It is a situation where an international coalition can reasonably hope to act together to check the ambitions of a dangerous man and a mistaken nation.

As imperfect as the U.S. record is in dealing with the world, I believe there is a case for a sober willingness to use U.S. power in this instance. That judgment may or may not be right. History will judge that. But it was a sober and considered judgment, made while Congress was debating the issue in advance, not after the fact while the troops are in the field.

I believe there is a chance here, through collective action by a broad range of countries, to make the Middle East a less dangerous place and to make the world a little safer. The role the United Nations has played is important. The international consensus that Saddam Hussein had to be challenged directly with force is constructive. The tough call, of course, was the one that Congress had to confront directly in its pre-Jan. 16 debate: Had the alternatives to war been reasonably tested? It is my conviction that the president was right in believing that delay served no purpose and might in fact have permitted Iraq to succeed in breaking up the international coalition and defeating the international campaign against him.

Those judgments are certainly subject to challenge, even while the troops are in the field and under fire. One of the great benefits of our system is that people don't have to accept the judgment of one president or one editor. I respect those who come to a different conclusion about what conscience requires. And I certainly fear that the U.S. military, now permitted to use the gadgets that it has built over the years, may learn the wrong lessons from the successes those weapons at least initially brought. If there are reasons to question whether the American people have learned the right "lessons of Vietnam," there are also reasons to fear that the generals and the military-industrial complex will learn the wrong "lessons of Iraq."

For now, though, I do not see that happening. The president has been restrained and balanced in his assessment of the risks and the issues. The generals, especially Gen. Colin Powell, have been extraordinarily alert to such issues as cultural and religious sensitivities and the risk to civilians. I may doubt whether we can truly create anything as grandiose as a "new world order," any more than we could "make the world safe for democracy." Utopianism and excessive optimism have often been a peculiarly American curse. But we do have some chance of making the world a little safer, and we may be able to make it clear just how dangerous and wrong Saddam Hussein's leadership has been.

As much as I understand the passion and conviction of those who learned from Vietnam that the use of force is always and everywhere wrong, or that it is wrong in this particular case, I am glad that the United States was able to act against Iraq. I will never be a lover of war. I hope this war will be mercifully brief and that its objectives can be controlled. I hope we will do more of what ought to be done afterward to diminish the risk of the recurrence of war. I believe that this country was not wrong, though, to believe that the time had come to take a stand and to act.

Hope shines, but utopia is elusive

This remarkable August to which we have just said good-bye, like August of 1914, has left a world radically changed.

This time, we almost hope it will be changed for the better.

In 1914, there was the sense of loss, of a world sliding into war, of the end of what the popular historian Barbara Tuchman called Europe's long golden summer afternoon. "The lamps are going out all over Europe," said Sir Edward Grey, then Britain's foreign secretary, as the world slipped into war, "and we shall not see them lit again in our generation."

This time, there is the sense that the change is for the better, that the great tyranny that arose out of the wreckage of the old order in the era of World War I is now itself dying, that such ideas as democracy and the consent of the governed have become newly potent. Woodrow Wilson's notion of the self-determination of peoples, too, looks less like a relic of misplaced idealism and more like a concept that is driving the struggles of ethnocentric and freedom-craving peoples everywhere.

Sept. 1, 1991

It is a time for hope. It ought to be a time when we remember how often in human history we have vanquished one tyranny and found not liberation but disillusionment.

Will this new world truly be better? We Americans love the idea of human progress and the hope of utopia almost as much as we tend to celebrate heroes. Even now, after the disillusionment so often visited upon us by the 20th Century, we still have a president who dreams and talks aloud of a new world order, somehow safer, more nearly just, more hopeful. A new world order!

I am haunted by the thought that our love of heroes and our hope for utopia will get us into trouble again. We discover that Mikhail Gorbachev is not, after all, really larger than life, and we create a Boris Yeltsin to take his place. We watch the death throes of the dogmatic utopianism of the Marxists, and we dare to dream of a democratic promised land in which the lambs will lie down with the lions and not be eaten.

We say our benedictions over the supernationalist vision of the communists and find joy in the renewed stirrings of nationalists everywhere, even though we can see in the present and in the past what tribalism has so often done in Europe.

In so many ways, it is as though the last 75 years had never happened. The titanic struggle of this century has ended with the collapse of the communist empire and the re-emergence of all the other struggles — national, tribal, religious — that were submerged in the era of the Cold War.

The countries around the Atlantic lake, led by the United States, spent their resources furiously to meet the challenge of communism, and they did it. They demonstrated that Marxism, even more than most other utopian schemes, was morally bankrupt and destructive of the human spirit. They showed that the liberation of individuals, rather than the harnessing of communities, is our best hope for human society.

We in this country still don't always fully appreciate what powerful ideas are embodied in the political thought that shaped the American revolution. People around the world are dying for such ideas as the consent of the governed, the worth of the individual, the liberating power of the marketplace, the vitality of a system of due process. Here, such ideas often seem like the stale stuff of history books.

Over the last few years, I've been able to travel to a lot of odd corners around the world. It is energizing to hear people who are not yet free talk of what it means to be free: in South Africa, in Chile before the plebiscite, in El Salvador on the one hand and Nicaragua on the other, on a train in the Soviet Union and in a tiny apartment in Czechoslovakia. I've come to a new level of distrust of systems that are supposed to save us from ourselves, and faith in individuals and ideals operating within a constitutional system.

The American society can be proud of the role it has played in exposing the fraud that was communism and in liberating the human community from that particular tyranny. Our ideals are the ones being celebrated around the world as August slides into September in the year 1991. We also need to ask ourselves how we, too, can and should celebrate those ideals and put them to work, the better to liberate our own society.

More than summer is dying now. The framework within which the people of the world have lived out their lives for the last half century and in some ways the last three-quarters of a century has been torn asunder.

It is a time for hope. It ought to be a time when we remember how often in human history we have vanquished one tyranny and found not liberation but disillusionment. We ought to remember how many dark nights there have been in this century and how hard it is to keep alive the hopes of humankind.

There are still a lot of lamps to be relit.

Get beyond hopelessness in Mideast

If you are Israeli and you have lived all your life in a state of siege, if you have been haunted by individual or collective memories of the Holocaust, if you are a veteran of several wars and of lonely frontier duty, your reluctance to believe that peace has a chance is not hard to understand.

If you are Palestinian and you have seen the Israeli army batter down the houses of suspected participants in the *intifada*, if you have spent all your life without rights in your own land, if you have seen your dreams of statehood booted around by supposed friend and enemy alike, then you, too, understandably find it hard to believe that the peacemakers have your best interests at heart.

If you are an American Jew and have vowed "never again" and have invested your hopes for the deliverance of your people in the state of Israel, you, too, are probably wary. And if you are an American of Arab origin and have identified with the victimization of the Palestinians, how can you possibly take hope?

Nov. 3, 1991

Dare you hope? Dare you think that there might be common ground? Dare you believe that George Bush and James Baker really have no agenda in the Middle East but peace?

Yet here is the president of the United States telling you that the Middle East has in fact been changed. Here is the U.S. secretary of state, plodding doggedly back and forth among the parties, alternately frightening you and giving you hope, insisting that it is your duty to humanity to give peace a chance. Dare you hope? Dare you think that there might be common ground? Dare you believe that George Bush and James

Baker really have no agenda in the Middle East but peace?

Do the rest of you, those with no direct ethnic ties to the Arab-Israeli conflict, dare to believe that your country can play the role of honest broker? Do you have reason to believe it is worth your president's while, when the poor here are crying for mercy and the cities are pained and the middle class is squeezed, to be trying to arrange a deal between people who feel so threatened by the prospect of a deal?

George Bush and James Baker are betting that there are changes in the Middle East and in the world that make this a moment when there might be opportunity, when there might be hope. They have been accused by some of the partisans of thinking merely that they can somehow bully the parties (or particularly one or the other side) into an agreement. I think that argument is wrong. I believe the president and the secretary of state are right. I believe this is one of those moments when you must try to catch the tide of change and move with it.

So what is different? Why now?

■ First, the world equation is different. The Soviet Union now clearly is a great power only in the fiction of international relations, a polite fiction usually maintained by George Bush because it has its uses. The secretary of state, on one of the Sunday talk shows, spoke more candidly: There is only one Great Power now, in a diplomatic sense. Around the world, regional conflicts fed by the struggle between East and West are suddenly more open to solution.

■ The Soviet Union is not merely weaker, but its struggling leaders, and especially Mikhail Gorbachev, actually seem to want to be helpful in settling conflicts their predecessors once stoked. The Soviet Union has been trying to make historic amends to the Israelis and to Jews and seems no longer eager or able to trade on the resentments in the Arab world.

■ Despite the fact that the Persian Gulf War ended with Saddam Hussein still in power, the war did fundamentally alter the balance of power in the Middle East. Iraq, while still a potential threat to Israel, is much less so. Syria, deprived of its Soviet patron, knows it must find a new role in the world and the Middle East. Jordan knows that its king's role as the Artful Dodger of the Middle East has virtually played out. Egypt and Saudi Arabia, though far from free of their historic animosities and the pressures within the Arab world, have more freedom and more confidence than in the past. Lebanon's bitter civil war is being suppressed, for better or for worse, and is being replaced by Syrian oversight. And above all, the region has seen what a mighty, swift sword the United States can bring to bear when it chooses to do so.

■ Israel is facing both the best of times and the worst of times in its historic alliance with the United States. For the first time, during the Persian Gulf War, American soldiers were literally defending Israel on Israeli soil. U.S. force came down on the head of one of Israel's worst enemies. Yet at the same time, it is clear that this American president at least is not willing to treat the Israeli connection as the sole American interest in the Middle East. U.S. patience with the status quo in the Middle East has been strained.

■ Within Israel, there is a sense that something different has to be done about the Palestinian question, that somehow there has to be an answer more consistent with the moral values of the Israeli people. The *intifada* may be wearing down, but there is also some Israeli weariness with the uneasy role of occupying army.

■ Among the Palestinians themselves, there seems also to be weariness with the struggle and at least some greater readiness to try a more conciliatory approach.

Will these changes and others bring peace? The odds are still against it. The seeds of conflict were planted long ago in the soil of the Middle East. People who have demonized and dehumanized each other do not easily turn to healing.

Surely, though, enough is changed that there is plenty of reason to try. You do not have to be possessed by the demon of anti-Jewish bias to see the Palestinians as victims whose cry of pain needs to be answered. You do not have to be a Holocaust survivor to believe that the world needs to keep its word to people who have sought refuge in the Jewish homeland. And you do not have to be some fuzzy-minded do-gooder to believe that there can be a basis on which the swords in the Middle East can indeed be beaten into plowshares.

In South Africa, hope replaces tyranny

When my younger brother asked, with honest puzzlement, why I would want to go to South Africa, I answered — somewhat huffily, I daresay: "Because there's a revolution going on there, and because I'm a journalist."

Afterward, I regretted my pomposity and wondered about my presumption. And yet ... and yet, there is no story on Earth right now more gripping, more touching, or more worthy of our sympathetic attention. South Africa, so long the country so many Americans have loved to hate, is now caught up in a drama of epic proportions.

Indeed, the story is so full of poignant themes that it is hard not to turn it into melodrama. To the extent that we can hope to understand the struggle as something more than a cliché, the beauty of the story is often in the subtlety and complexity.

The story centers on a piece of real estate as consistently beautiful as any other in the world. I had been there once before and thought it beautiful then. I

JUNE 7, 1992

There is a chance in South Africa that this beloved country can be redeemed and held together by something more enduring than the bonds of oppression.

underestimated its magic. Cape Town, near the Cape of Good Hope, is one of the more hauntingly beautiful places I have seen. Riding a bus from Johannesburg to Kruger National Park, or the famous Blue Train from Johannesburg to Cape Town, you sense the vast ruggedness of South Africa as a whole.

The story of the people is more subtle, more complicated than we imagine. The world has focused — quite accurately, I think — on the story of the evil apartheid system and the outlaw status of previous South African governments.

I think apartheid ranks right up there among the 20th Century's chamber-of-horrors stories: with the massacre of the Armenians, the Holocaust, the Killing Fields of Cambodia, with the massacre of the Kurds. It was, and its remnants are, an unspeakable horror.

But if it was important to see clearly the evil that apartheid represented — with its tyranny, with its often vile racism, with its police-state machinery — it is important not to turn this story into simpleminded melodrama.

There were the heroes all along — black and white — who tried, at great risk, to redeem their beloved country: the Alan Patons, the Nadine Gordimers, the Nelson Mandelas, the Albie Sachs, the Steve Bikos, the Helen Sussmans. I think of my friend Gerald Shaw, the assistant editor of the Cape Times, who spoke six years ago of being a South African as like living with a perpetual toothache. I found South Africa more hopeful this time and more free; I marveled that Shaw had stayed on and fought for so long, against such odds, to reclaim and restore the rule of law and the claims of decency.

If there have been heroes all along, major and minor, named and unnamed, the scene today is dominated by two even more amazing figures: Nelson Mandela and F.W. de Klerk. South Africa is a more hopeful place today because these two extraordinary men emerged, each from his own confinement, to forge a partnership that may just redeem this place.

Nelson Mandela's story may be the most incredible of them all: a man who emerges from 27 years in prison with discipline and character and more forgiveness in his heart than I could have mustered.

F.W. de Klerk, though, is quite a story in himself: the creature of the system, the faithful National Party servant, who steps unblinking into the sunlight of opportunity, who knows intuitively how to move to transform the politics of his situation. I think we don't yet know the limits of de Klerk's vision; inevitably, you wonder at the Gorbachev parallel and whether he could, indeed, understand just how much South Africa must change. So far, so good, though; he has been proving himself immensely resourceful in seizing the day.

South Africans speak with almost disturbing consistency about the inevitability of this process and about the new South Africa that will emerge "at the end of the day." It is a far, far more hopeful place than I saw when I was there six years ago, and yet I do not believe a happy ending is inevitable. Tragedy moves with a seemingly inevitable logic, too.

Yet South Africans — many, many South Africans, black and white — are daring to let themselves hope now. They hope for an end to the evil of the past — both to colonialism and to the bloodlust for revenge against colonialism. They dare to speak, many of them, of a new day for themselves, a new day for South Africa and for all of Africa.

There are plenty of voices of dissent and doubt and nostalgia for the world that is slowly giving way. You can make a case for pessimism.

But there is a chance in South Africa that this beloved country can be redeemed and held together by something more enduring than the bonds of oppression. That struggle, I'm here to tell you, is as dramatic as any fiction that you could devise.

There's a revolution going on, and the last chapters are still to be written.

RACE

From Orval Faubus to Nelson Mandela

Broken dreams and the problem of race

The summer sun was hot, and he seemed old, though he had small children trailing him through the fields.

I was a college student, barely 19, and I was white, and he was black. What was more, I had a summer job as a cotton acreage checker for the U.S. Department of Agriculture, which made me official.

We had gone over the boundaries of his fields, marking them off on an aerial photograph of his farm. His was one of those farms created by Franklin Roosevelt's farm community program, and he was one of the farmers who had survived the Depression and the war. He was a good farmer and a man of dignity.

When we had finished measuring the land, we sat down under a tree to fill out the form. I wrote it all out, computed the acreage, and finally turned to him and asked if he would sign the form.

For an awful moment he hesitated, embarrassed and ashamed. "I'll have to make my X," he said, "I can't write my name."

The moment troubled me, and I, too, hesitated, not knowing what to say.

Nov. 16, 1975

Like the flame in a black-smith's forge, the problem of race has twisted the steel of our cities and reshaped the maps of our metropolitan areas. It has made beasts of otherwise decent men and made cowards of us all.

Then, perhaps sensing my discomfort, he asked to be remembered to my father, whom he knew, and spoke of my grandfather, who was dead. Then he spoke of himself and his children.

"It hasn't been so good for me," he said. "Maybe it hasn't been so good either for your father and your grandfather, too. We haven't all known just how to get along.

"But these children," he said, "these children will have it different. They'll go to school, and they'll learn, and they'll come to get along.

"One day you'll have children, and maybe your children and my children will be different from us, and things will be different for them."

And the world — I thought with hope — will measure a man by what he is and will give children a future with hope and a childhood without bitterness. The Joe Larkins of this world — I still remember his name — will not stand humiliated before some pink-cheeked college kid with a new blue Chevrolet pickup and a government document in his hand.

The memory of that July morning came back to me later when I heard Martin Luther King Jr. speak of his dream of the day when the little black children and the little white children would play together on the red clay hills of Georgia.

I thought of him this last week, too, when I read of the east-side Detroit black family who had a cross burned on its lawn. I thought of him when the dispute over the DeMascio school desegregation order broke out into the open last week. I thought of him when a gang of black toughs beat up some white kids outside Detroit's Osborn High School.

I am afraid we have not done too well by Mr. Larkin's dream or Martin Luther King's or mine. We haven't made it very far from the cotton patch yet, and I'm not sure I know the way.

The problem of race — the problem that lay back of my encounter with Mr. Larkin 20 years ago — remains the great unresolved problem of the American society.

Like the flame in a blacksmith's forge, it has twisted the steel of our cities and reshaped the maps of our metropolitan areas. It has made beasts of otherwise decent men and made cowards of us all.

Until we can face it — until we can learn to live with the awful truth about ourselves and with the mixed truth about those who differ from us — our cities and our stomachs will churn and sicken us.

The issue may not be Detroit tomorrow. It may be the near suburbs, and then the far suburbs. Today downtown, tomorrow Northland, the next day the far suburban malls. The battlegrounds on which we struggle with ourselves are not selected with predictable precision.

Why, then, can we not deal with it now, here, today? With white fears and black anxiety? With white prejudice and black distrust? With the truth that we do not have one nation indivisible, with liberty and justice and all those other good things?

Unless we can start — unless we can learn to deal with each other as people to people, as neighbor to neighbor — then the big birthday party next year will be a big joke. And we who believed — with Joe Larkin — in an American dream will be of all men most to be pitied.

The great migration from farmlands

In summer, the dust lay deep on the road that followed the bayou from our house, past the lane, past my grandparents' house, past Lee Rainey's house, past the pond and the graveyard to Mr. Sam Whitlock's store at the highway.

The dust burned your bare feet as you walked, though here and there the shade of a tree made it refreshingly cool. Sometimes the dust hid a thorn from the trees along the road, a hazard to bare feet.

My grandparents' house was old and fading, a rambling old farmhouse with a central hall.

The old house is gone now, destroyed in a fire, and only a pear tree marks where once the house and the barns and the commissary stood. Now are only fields, planted to the road's edge, machine-efficient and irrigated.

Lee Rainey's house was perhaps a quarter-mile further up the road. It was weathered, too; so far as I could tell, it never knew paint. The porch ran the length of the front and sagged.

JAN. 9, 1976

What we have in the cities is nothing more nor less than America's last best chance to rise above the problem of race.

The fence that surrounded his house was irregular, totally unlike the whitewashed rail fence Lee built to my father's specifications around our house. Not much money for Lee Rainey's fence.

Lee Rainey was a sharecropper who tried to scratch out a living on someone else's land while paying crop rent and operating on a kind of credit and barter system. It evolved in the cash-poor rural South after the Civil War. While it did provide a crude basis on which the economy could operate, its effect was often cruel, and it helped a rigid class structure to survive in the South for a long time.

Despite the effects of that system, Lee Rainey was an awesome figure to me: He sometimes let me drive the team and wagon; he indulged my wish to work in the garden and the field; he let me fish with him; he taught me how to drive a nail.

As mechanization came to the farm, and as wartime and postwartime brought reports and rumors of jobs in the cities, more and more of the sharecropper families left, heading north, heading west.

Lee Rainey was one of the last to leave. He asked my father for land to build a church, and he hung on long after his children had begun to drift away. Finally, he went to Kansas, where Joe and L.T. and Clara had gone.

I liked Lee Rainey as a man.

It occurred to me then, at an early age, how strange the sharecropper system was. No one made a lot of money, and a landowner was likely to live only relatively well. But what an archaic system sharecropping was, how unfair, how little chance there was for anyone to better himself or his children.

That system had to collapse, and eventually it did. The coming of machinery in the years after World War II made it uneconomic.

In any case, the Lee Raineys of this country became a part of one of the greatest and most poignant mass migrations in history. That migration and its impact both on the rural United States and on our cities are among the more profound facts of the 20th Century.

That migration is also, to me at least, having seen it from both ends, one of the saddest aspects of our American democracy. The former rural poor were downtrodden by a system that seemed almost feudal in its rigidity and structure. It was decidedly evil and had to change.

So the Lee Raineys left, leaving their cows, pursuing their hopes to the cities, accepting as truth the promise that things would be better "up North." For those who were black, as Lee was, the cities often meant not good jobs and opportunity, but frustration and emptiness. Lacking skills, they glutted the labor market and strained the services.

That great migration dribbled to an end in the mid-'60s, as the population pool in the rural South was drained almost dry. The cities have been struggling for these 10 years to come to terms with that population shift and all it meant. They have made some headway, but progress is slow.

And the nation has been slow to recognize the special burdens placed on cities in trying to set aright injustices and social maladies that were 300 years in the making. The cities themselves have been slow to change and respond to the needs of a people so long oppressed.

What we have in the cities, though, is nothing more nor less than America's last best chance to rise above the problem of race: to make cities again places of hope, to create an ever-larger black middle class, to overcome both fear and bitterness, to share power, to find a basis for peace among all of us.

Will we do it? The returns are still out, I think. Time slips away. The recession hasn't helped.

And the unresolved question of how we handle that great migration and its result may well be the ultimate test of whether our society endures and overcomes. It is a question that we answer every day, by what we do in Detroit.

Hope shines from city's black churches

It was a sublime summer Sunday morning — a carbon copy of so many other sublime Michigan summer mornings.

The soft breeze riffled through the cottonwoods and willows. The air was warm, but velvet smooth.

Out in the rolling lake country of Oakland County, the sunlight shattered into a thousand pieces as it hit the surface of the water.

People were doing quiet human things: going to the beaches, heading for the drugstore for a paper, going to church.

On Rosa Parks Blvd. in Detroit, the same sun played hide-and-seek with the shadows there.

Here and there, one could see the signs of what we euphemistically call the urban problem: a broken window, a vandalized building, an assortment of rubble-strewn lots.

But here, too, on a Sunday morning, there was the tranquility of a golden Michigan day. Here, too, there were people doing quiet Sunday-morning kinds of things: going to church, walking the neighborhood, tending the house or the lawn.

JULY 2, 1978

These people — the black church people of America — impress me still, as their counterparts often did in the '50s and '60s, as among the more heroic people of the world.

This happened to be a Sunday morning when I was making a talk — on "Men's Day" — to the people at the Greater Quinn AME Church.

The sanctuary was a place of peace and beauty amid the clatter of the city. It was warm inside — the air-conditioning was installed but not yet working — and the congregation was friendly.

The minister, noting I had grown up in Arkansas, asked how many of the congregation had grown up in Arkansas. A good dozen or more people stood up.

I talked of justice and violence and hope and the city. The crowd seemed attentive.

In the responses of the congregation, and the comments afterward, I was struck by the forbearance and the Christian charity of the people. These people — the black church people of America — impress me still, as their counterparts often did in the '50s and '60s, as among the more heroic people of the world.

There is a moral power — Dr. Martin Luther King Jr. knew it and used it — that comes from being black, knowing the racial flaw in the fabric of America, and yet reaching out a hand in reconciliation.

Now, it seems to me, there is a degree of hopefulness on Rosa Parks Blvd., formerly 12th Street. Oh, I know the real social dynamite is not locked up in the breasts of the people inside the church. It is in the alienated young on the outside — the outside of the church, the outside of the society.

But do not underestimate the growing power and sense of destiny of the emerging black middle class — people gaining political power, getting economic opportunity, learning to cope with the white man's America.

And do not underestimate the strength of a religious and cultural heritage that provides much to build on in building a reconciled society. There is a common yearning for peace, for order, for reconciliation that gives us much to work with.

Michigan, moreover, is a good place to work with these building blocks. Despite the sordidness and bleakness of much of the industrial concentration we have built in southeast Michigan, this is a state that has opened up opportunity for a multitude over the years.

In some ways, I think southeast Michigan is the most American of places: for good and bad, for violent failure and golden opportunity. We have to hammer out here some kind of accommodation among all the racial and cultural strains that make up a great metropolitan area.

I came back from Europe this spring more convinced than ever that the burden of history is squarely on us, that there aren't any tidy little models that tell us what to do to make the American dream real. We have to fashion our own solutions out of our own complex cultural mosaic.

On a sun-dappled Sunday morning, approaching the Fourth of July, I almost believe we can do it. I know that the contrasts and the inequities say it will not be easy.

I know, too, though, that the residual goodwill and decency of so many people say we have to try harder.

The revolution a schoolgirl started

It was a glorious day, as I remember it, that May afternoon in 1954.

But, then, they all seemed glorious that spring. We were freshmen then, and we had just started dating in the very early spring, and we reveled in it.

What both of us remember of that day is my coming to Galloway Hall, the freshman girls' dorm, to pick her up. The headline in the afternoon paper in the reception area told of the Supreme Court's decision in a case involving a black schoolgirl from Topeka, Kan.

Separate but equal was inherently unequal, the court said, and therefore illegal.

We remember talking with others, then, about what it might mean. As we recall, most of the students were glad but uncertain what it meant. Later, my father said he thought the "thinking people" could work it out. We knew it meant momentous change, but what?

From east of the Mississippi, the protest was vehement. Some demagogues began to denounce it in Arkansas.

May 20, 1979

Brown vs. Board of Education may not be precisely relevant in Detroit, but the revolution it started in the South is. Change is. Racial reconciliation is. The empowerment of blacks is.

The governor said we were law-abiding people, as I remember it.

So we felt okay. Troubled by headlines that talked of "race-mixing," but okay. We would work it out.

So we went out to the dining hall, to the library, to the movies maybe. It was almost final exam time. There were other things to think about, immediate things, each other.

It did not hit me until late this past week. Twenty-five years since Brown. Twenty-five years since we started to date. The great events of those years are intertwined so with the personal events of our lives. I wish I had kept a diary.

Maybe I can remember some of the highlights:

■ November 1956. The Arkansas elections that year were full of scary talk from racial demagogues. The words had an angry, buzz-saw quality to them: "defiance," "interposition," even "rebellion." I remember going with her to the polling place to cast a "maiden" vote (under the old poll tax system, the first, or maiden, vote was free). The demagogues lost. Orval Faubus wasn't much of a governor, maybe, but at least he didn't seem a demagogue. And he wanted to build schools.

■ September 1957. This was the day my bride and I were leaving Arkansas for New Orleans, for graduate school. We read the papers with confusion, bewilderment. Gov. Faubus had called out the National Guard to prevent the integration of the schools in Little Rock. I wish I could say I understood instantly the enormity of his act of rebellion. I didn't. Only later did I fully sense the cynicism and danger in what he did.

■ July 1958. We go back home for a visit. The grandparents are pleased with the new baby. I am shocked by what I find at home. Politics is a prairie fire. Faubus now plays the demagogue. Every encounter seems to turn into a political argument. The mood is defiant; the power of the Faubus machine is overweening. There is no middle ground left on race. There is a new tension.

■ Early 1959. I board a city bus or street car in New Orleans. There is a notice that separation of the races on public conveyances is illegal and now forbidden. The old signs are down. I hesitate between a seat beside a black person and one by a white, indecisive. A Catholic schoolgirl in her uniform marches to her seat beside the black, breaking the color line, starting the change. I am embarrassed and shamed at my hesitation. "A little child shall lead them."

■ June 1959. Graduate school done, we return to Arkansas. The subject of race hangs heavy over the state. Little Rock remains in turmoil. I cover a desegregation case involving a small suburban district called Dollarway. Even reporting in itself seems to bear its risks. There are threats, angry meetings, rumors of the Klan, ugly phone calls. But the moderates are starting to rally in Little Rock, and a few more surface even in the eastern, cotton-country part of the state.

■ July 1960. A leave of absence from the paper, a job as press secretary in a campaign for governor against Orval Faubus' bid for a fourth term. The campaign is futile, but political change is starting to take hold. The voters defeat a state school-closing amendment. Now it seems strange and faraway, but there was a time when people talked of abolishing schools. But it was stopped. The schools were saved in a vote that November.

■ August 1963. We are vacationing in a national forest, beside a clear creek. The fishing is poor, but I catch one beautiful bass. The children are small; we are with friends. On the way out, the radio tells of the peaceful and beautiful March on Washington. A friend who went tells us that in Arkansas, too, we shall overcome. Faubus remains in power, but change has started. Integration is becoming a fact. The defiance slowly ebbs away.

■ Summer 1964. A move to North Carolina. The Civil Rights Act is settling many of the old questions. Lyndon Johnson, a Southerner, is leading. School integration is spreading. Tension is high. Some of our trips home, driving straight through Georgia and Alabama, leave us uneasy. We drive all night. Alabama's dark roads seem threatening, alive with danger. Back home, the talk isn't demagogues anymore; it is Republicans. Could Winthrop Rockefeller really win the governorship? He eventually does.

■ 1965. The talk now is voting rights. The Voting Rights Act of 1965 provokes talk of "conquered provinces," but it works. Southern politics is altered forever. Blacks vote. Coalitions form. Attitudes change.

■ Summer 1967. We are to host a visitor from Africa for dinner. I go to the home of Winston-Salem's black school board member to pick her up. Waiting for the visitor in the living room of his home, talking to his daughter, we watch the television news. The screen is full of flames. Detroit is burning. Will there ever be racial peace? It is not a time of hope. Still, change goes on. The courts grind ahead.

■ Summer 1968. We are in Detroit now. A city without newspapers, without hope, without effective leadership, with racial passions as angry and intractable as any I ever saw in the South. Does Brown have relevance here? Is change possible? It seems so heavy.

The diary could go on, but most of you can fill in the rest. Brown vs. Board of Education may not be precisely relevant in Detroit, but the revolution it started in the South is. Change is. Racial reconciliation is. The empowerment of blacks is.

The society still has a long way to go to be the truly open and accessible America we said we wanted. Racism is still with us, insidious and painful. Violence and conflict always imperil the law.

Still, this quarter century has brought more constructive change than many others to American life. Cities almost dare to hope again that they, too, might somehow overcome. Not always in the ways we thought, not always surefootedly. But overcome, nonetheless.

'We shall overcome' … someday, maybe

When they marched and sang, that August in 1963, there was not much doubt who held the moral high ground.

In a land contorted by institutionalized racism, where the harsh edge of racial conflict rubbed and tore at the fabric of society, here was this young Alabama black man talking of redemption.

"I have a dream …," he cried. "We shall overcome …," the crowd sang. A friend of mine from Little Rock, Irene Samuel, later gave me a record of the program at the Lincoln Memorial that August day, including the "I have a dream" speech. The album cover was entitled "We Shall Overcome." To that she added this inscription, "In Arkansas, too — someday."

I was not ashamed then, and I am not ashamed now, to say which side I was on. I believed then, and I believe now, that the way we have dealt with the problem of race is the tragic flaw in the American dream. I knew then, and I know now, that unless we can overcome the heritage of slavery and the subtler substitutes that replaced it, we will continue to endanger ourselves and our society.

AUG. 28, 1983

The way we have dealt with the problem of race is the tragic flaw in the American dream.

The objectives in August 1963 were much more readily identifiable than they are now. Voting discrimination. Discrimination in public accommodations. Segregation by law and practice. Unchecked brutality by whites against blacks under the guise of law and order.

Life was cheapened by the prevailing attitudes. I remember, as a young reporter working the police beat on a Saturday night in Pine Bluff, Ark., asking the desk sergeant what he had on the police reports.

"Just another nigger killing," he said. A life had been snuffed out, and that was how he dismissed it.

But what should I have expected? The very Constitution of the United States, I had been startled to discover in my history classes, had been hung up over the question of how to count slaves for purposes of representation. That constitutional convention, so capable of nobility on other questions, settled the issue by deciding that the slaves in the Southern states should be counted as three-fifths of a man. Imagine that. By Constitution, we decreed that they were less than men.

On the cotton farm where I grew, you could readily see — once the scales of self-deception were stripped from your eyes — what that meant. In the fields, black men and women worked from sunrise to sunset for a wage of $3 a day. The farmer rode in a blue Chevrolet pickup truck and spotted where the cotton choppers had missed anything. The schools might not be much for anyone, but in the white schools there were rudimentary science equipment and new book purchases. In the black schools, they learned of American democracy in secondhand books.

Ironically, it may have been those secondhand textbooks that saved us. I remember listening, during the latter part of the '60s, to one of the first candidate nights in North Carolina that included black candidates. The white candidates, I discovered, were talking about taxes and programs and assessments. The black candidates were talking of freedom and hope and the underlying principles of democracy. The contrast was striking.

All of that — both the institutionalized outrages and the heroic struggle of the civil rights movement — is seen now by too many people as being long ago and far away. The people of the Midwest never quite understood the degree to which they had been coconspirators in the preservation of racism. Many now are inclined to greet talk of the anniversary of this march as mere nostalgia or as something irrelevant to the great issues of our time.

The anger is there, the pain is there, the misunderstanding and hostility are there. Ours is still a racially divided and embittered society. It is not open and fluid and free, the way it ought to be. It does matter whether you are born black on the lower east side of Detroit or white in Oakland County.

And with the economic change that is overtaking us — with the high-tech revolution making many old-fashioned skills irrelevant and with too much of our educational system a disgrace — a good part of the black population sees no basis for hope. And the white population is less patient now than it was in the '60s with efforts to change these conditions.

So in considerable measure we are still talking about a dream, rather than a reality. Much has changed — in politics, in public life, in private attitudes. But much remains the same.

"I have a dream ...," he said. "We shall overcome ...," the crowd sang.

Maybe in Detroit, someday.

Distrust runs deep, but hope survives

The summer before I came to Detroit, I stood in the living room of one of the first black, public officials in Winston-Salem, N.C., and watched television film of Detroit burning.

I had gone to the home of Richard Erwin, then a member of the school board in that old Southern city, to pick up a guest — a visitor from Africa — to take her to dinner. She and I stood there, transfixed by the film of the flames of this great Northern city, for several paralyzing moments.

There we were — I, the white editorial page editor of Winston-Salem's daily papers, she, the black visitor from Africa, and the family of her host, a successful black lawyer just beginning to break through the harsh barriers of a Southern town. There we were, in the midst of a strained and studied act of international civility, watching a great American city burn. The years before had seemed to be years of hope and promise, years when

DEC. 8, 1985

I hope that it still counts for something to believe we are above all humans together, despite all that makes us hate each other.

we said "We shall overcome" and believed it. That moment seemed so full of despair.

Detroit had no special meaning for me then. In the early years of the civil rights revolution, I had always thought it was different "up there." Oh, I knew about the 1943 Detroit riot, and I knew it wasn't utopia. But I had naively believed that race was by then a predominantly Southern problem. If the problem of race could be surmounted in the South, I thought, the country could survive the crisis that the civil rights revolution in the South had laid bare.

By the summer of the next year, I had become a part of Detroit myself. I was drawn, first of all, by a much better job than I had had, but more than that, because I needed to try to understand better what was happening in the cities of this country. The history books hadn't quite prepared me for what I then understood about what was going on.

In the nearly 18 years since, as I have watched Detroit and Michigan struggle with the problem of race and with all the other problems of being an old, industrial society, there have been a lot of moments of despair and a lot of moments of hope. I know now, in a way that I only partly understood then, that the problem of race is a human tragedy, not just an American tragedy and certainly not just a Southern tragedy. My view of history is a lot less utopian now — I don't believe as much in final victories on this side of Jordan — and I know that the struggle to expurgate the racism in our society and in ourselves is more painful, more frustrating, more tedious than I thought as a very young man.

When I was a young man in Pine Bluff, Ark., I thought it might count for something that I went, along with maybe a half-dozen other whites, to a "Brotherhood Sunday" service at a black church. When I was a slightly older man in Little Rock, I thought it might help that I came to have black friends. When I was a young father on Detroit's northwest side, I thought maybe it was possible to help with the peaceful integration of a model middle school and thereby do something to mitigate the curse of race and racism.

I do not think it was wrong to have had such hopes then. I just underestimated the enemy within us. I did not understand the depths of society's fears — and mine. I did not comprehend what a burden fear and hatred and tradition and anger could be. I did not begin to know the twists and turns there would be on the road to a color-blind society.

There are those white folks today who think that if the black folks would just go away and let them be, this could be a pretty good society. There are those black folks today who would like to go away, to take refuge in their own kind of separatism. I believe just the opposite, that for better or for worse we are in this thing together.

This country is, for all its checkered history, a noble experiment. In the fragile world of human institutions, it has been a source of hope and strength. Detroit in many ways has been the archetypal American city, a place where people found a better life than they could have found wherever they came from. There is much to love and on the basis of which to build hope in both this country and this city.

The problem of race, though, has always been the soft underbelly of this country.

Still, I hope. I hope that it still counts for something to believe we are above all humans together, despite all that makes us hate each other.

On Friday morning, I got a letter from a black lawyer, Wiley Branton, whom I knew back in my Pine Bluff days. The first line of his letter began with these words, "Our mutual friend, Judge Damon Keith, requested that I send you … "

I don't mean to take refuge in the kind of hoary cliché that says "some of my best friends are … "

Still, I hope. I hope that we can learn, even this late in the history of this misbegotten human race, that we are brothers and sisters.

I hope that we can resist giving in to those who believe it is wrong to hope.

Guilt is poor basis for racial solutions

As we approach the end of the 1980s, it is hard to believe that guilt is a sufficient engine to drive this country to make amends for the historic wrongs done to blacks.

For that reason, I don't place a lot of faith in the call for reparations to black people as a way to set right these wrongs in our past. The nation backed quickly away from the idea of "40-acres-and-a-mule" for every freed slave in the 1860s. Given the history of the 1980s, it seems unlikely to do better now simply out of guilt.

If anything can persuade the American majority to make any continuing effort to assure full citizenship and the opportunity for full partnership for blacks in America, it will surely have to be not guilt but self-interest. This country needs to try to solve the problem of race in America because it cannot live with the fruits of its failure to do so thus far. This society will need educated black workers to cope with potential labor shortages as

APRIL 23, 1989

I continue to believe that there is enough enlightened self-interest and enough sense of shared humanity to enable us eventually to overcome our painful heritage.

early as the 1990s. It will need a conciliatory climate among the races if it is ever to make the society a less dangerous place. It needs racial cooperation to make our communities work.

Many whites during the 1980s have seemed to lose patience with the whole effort to set right the problem of race in America. Too many have lost faith in the notion that there can be constructive change. The argument that we have been merely practicing reverse discrimination has gained currency. Although many of our institutions — universities, businesses, public bodies — continue to struggle for diversity, white support for affirmative action and other presumed remedies seems to me to have been greatly diminished.

In such a context, I suspect, the City Council's call for reparations to be paid to blacks for the wrong done in slavery will, at least initially, tend to polarize an already polarized community even more. The white reaction that this is just one more "gimme" demand is almost predictable.

Is it impossible in such a context to get beyond trigger words such as "reparations" and to bring about constructive change? This country has tried to deal with such a concept, albeit imperfectly, with regard to Native American rights and the harm done to Japanese Americans during the relocation effort in World War II. But those were less threatening concessions for the white majority to make. The legacy of slavery is so massive, so bewildering, and so seemingly resistant to change.

Again, the best guide seems to me to be enlightened self-interest. You're going to pay coming or you're going to pay going. Michigan is now grappling with the biggest buildup in its prison system in history. The number of prisoners has more than doubled since Gov. James Blanchard came to office. A disproportionate number of those in prison are black. Would we not be better off spending the same money on early childhood education for needy people, especially blacks? On prenatal care? Can we never succeed in getting more young black people on promising career tracks and out of the violence and self-destruction of the ghetto streets? Can we not better spend our money on transportation to help inner-city young people get to where the jobs are?

You can call such efforts reparations if you like. You can also call them an investment in trying to assure that the vast majority of blacks get a full opportunity to buy into the society. I know the prison buildup was at least partially necessary, but in a very real sense, in doing it, we are bearing the costs of this society's past failures.

To change all this cannot, of course, be simply a matter of white self-interest or guilt. Blacks have an enormous self-interest in helping to assure that we overcome the destructive pathology that has taken over so many of the city's streets. Pride and a sense of self-reliance are indispensable parts of overcoming a historic pattern of discrimination.

I continue to believe that there is enough enlightened self-interest and enough sense of shared humanity to enable us eventually to overcome our painful heritage. The history of the world doesn't always inspire a lot of confidence that anyone can overcome the problem of race. No one ever said it would be easy, and no one should have ever said it could be a matter of white guilt or the compensation for past wrongs.

What we must say, again and again, is that we all have a vested interest in making this a society where people can live together in peace, hope, opportunity and mutual respect. And that we had better get on with it while there is yet time to overcome the past.

A story of contrasting lives

Nelson Mandela's remarkable day in Detroit on Thursday underscored, as few events have, the contrasts that confound anyone trying to describe the complex reality of this city.

The events at the Ford Rouge plant and at Tiger Stadium were rich in emotion and symbolism — especially, but certainly not exclusively, for black people. Surely Polish Americans, who so recently cheered the triumphal visit of Lech Walesa to this country, and Czechoslovak Americans, who were moved by the visit of Vaclav Havel to the United States, can identify with the emotional response Mr. Mandela's visit engendered among black Detroiters. If we are ever to overcome race in this country, we need to understand more about each other's heroes.

JULY 1, 1990

If we are ever to overcome race in this country, we need to understand more about each other's heroes.

And we in the media do have to try harder to understand the pride and the very real progress that many black people feel and see as endangered when we point out the sad other side of reality. We need to understand better that the story of the last 20 years in Detroit and in the United States really is a story of contrasts: of the proud, hopeful, articulate folk who filled Tiger Stadium Thursday, and of the angry, hopeless, voiceless sufferers who can be found within blocks of Tiger Stadium.

Two studies published in recent weeks have helped to put these contrasts into perspective. A group called the Business-Higher Education Forum, following a study cochaired by Clifton Wharton, former president of Michigan State University, issued a report on "The Three Realities of Minority Life in the

United States." It was a classic good news/bad news story. The good news is that one-third of all blacks and Hispanics in this country are now middle class and that the size of the black middle class has tripled over the last three decades. That's certainly a reality we in the press tend to obscure.

But the other two realities of minority life in this country are less reassuring: that a second one-third of the minority population in this country is underemployed and that a final third is becoming mired in the underclass — alienated, cut off from rewarding jobs, degraded too often by violence and drugs.

When we in the media insist on describing those parts of the reality of life in the United States, we are accused of accentuating the negative.

The '80s left many Americans, whites as well as blacks, convinced that if we just quit talking about America's failures, they would somehow go away. I think, though, even as we celebrate both Nelson Mandela and Detroit, we had better find ways to change the reality in which that lower two-thirds of black Americans find themselves struggling.

That's where a second report comes in — one cochaired by Ray Marshall and Bill Brock, both of them former secretaries of labor — which attempts to grapple with "America's Choice: High Skills or Low Wages." It essentially argues that in our attempts to be competitive internationally we have badly neglected the skills of the bottom 70 percent of our population, while we concentrated on reforming the education of the college-bound upper 30 percent. And over the last two decades, we have achieved growth by expanding the work force.

This study points out that, with the work force no longer able to grow, we are going to have to increase productivity or see our economy fail to compete.

The Marshall-Brock report argues that the nation needs to create a system of employment and training boards to oversee a new high-performance education and training system. It argues, as does the Business-Higher Education Forum, that there is a powerful economic interest in changing the status and training of this bottom two-thirds of U.S. workers. Because we face the prospect of growing labor shortages, we have to try to upgrade the skills of this part of the population.

Detroit in particular has been a place that did not value education for everyone because the experience of so many families said it was unimportant. But our failure to understand the changing demands for skills has left this city behind in adapting to the demands of international competition and of the need for productivity growth. The result is that, while some prosper, many sink into low-income jobs or drop out of the job market altogether.

Although we ought to celebrate the real progress made by the black middle class that is emerging in Detroit, we ought to wrestle more effectively with that other reality, with the people who are being left behind and left out, a disproportionate number of them black. We can't change the conditions they face by public relations gimmicks or mirrors. We have to find ways to encourage the reliance on skills, rather than cheap labor, and to help those who have been left behind to develop the skills they need. If we don't deal with that reality more effectively and more honestly, we will find it harder to enjoy our shining moments, even in a well-secured stadium or an insulated suburban home.

That, too, is a part of the reality of Detroit in this summer of 1990.

'So which side were you on, Dad?'

He will not be 9 until next month, and I would not have guessed that he would be drawn into the TV docudrama "Separate but Equal."

In fact, he had come to sit on the bed where I was watching it last Monday evening more as a way of stalling his own departure to bed than anything else. I was going away for a few days the next day, and he wasn't very sleepy, and, well, it just seemed nice to sit close for a little while.

As he sat there, though, he was drawn into the dramatization of the battle over school desegregation, and he was full of questions. He had been to some historic sites lately, and he had heard about slavery and the Underground Railway, and he seemed to understand a surprising amount about the struggle within and before the U.S. Supreme Court.

I told him that the court decision had come down when I was in college in Arkansas. I kept saying things out loud about how long ago some of it seemed and how coercive the atmosphere had been.

As the court and its justices wrestled with the old separate-but-equal doctrine that had been the law of this land, as we relived the intense struggle over whether the court should confront the moral imperative or take a narrow view of the law, I was pained to remember how evil American apartheid had been.

As the drama built toward the decisive moment, Jon turned to me and asked, innocently and with simple, honest curiosity, "Which side were you on, Dad?"

> **APRIL 14, 1991**
>
> *We have to remind ourselves that the question of justice in America still is, at its root, a moral question, a question of whether we can build a society of opportunity and fairness.*

As the drama built toward the decisive moment, Jon turned to me and asked, innocently and with simple, honest curiosity, "Which side were you on, Dad?"

For my generation in the South, those were days when we had to choose, but when the pressures were pretty unbelievable. I remember the fear I felt, not even for taking sides, but for simply reporting the truth during my cub reporter days. I remember some times when I kept silent and hesitated, and I regret those. But mostly I'm glad I can tell my son that somehow I understood what was at stake and why things had to change.

It has been more than 30 years since those days, but I can remember one night when I thought to myself, "I am 23 years old, and I may never again be quite so sure as I am right now which side to be on."

The years since have shown that the issues that seemed so simple did have some subtleties that maybe I didn't see then. But in those days, there was nothing subtle about the fundamental issue. The question before the nation was simple and straightforward: How could this Republic profess democratic ideals and still sanction the notion that some of its people were second-class citizens? And how could we have possibly kidded ourselves that there really could be such a thing as "separate but equal"?

In the years since, as we have struggled with the unfulfilled promise of the American Revolution, we have often seemed to lose our way. The struggle for justice and democracy has turned out to be harder than a lot of us expected then. As the civil rights struggle moved beyond the question of segregation by law, we discovered that race in America is a much, much tougher problem than I had thought it was back then.

Surely, though, we have to remind ourselves that the question of justice in America still is, at its root, a moral question, a question of whether we can build a society of opportunity and fairness. A lot of people no longer believe we can, or they no longer care. We need to be reminded, again and again, that how we deal with each other is still not right, is still not fair. We all have to struggle with the legacy of this country's early reluctance to try to overcome the burden of our history. I was glad to see television trying to confront that defining moment in our history. I was glad my son seemed to understand as much as he did. I'm glad he cared to ask where I was during those days.

All of us, children and aging adults alike, need to know that life matters, that we care about and stand for something, that our lives really do need to be undergirded by some sort of concern for moral principles. The time surely comes in all our lives when someone with trusting brown eyes turns to us and says, "Which side were you on, Dad?"

There isn't one among us who can always answer that kind of question with satisfaction and honor. We're human, and there will be times when we will look back and know that we didn't do nearly well enough at understanding what the moral imperatives were at some of the crucial moments in our lives.

Still, in these moments when what is right seems so often unclear, when the sense of individual obligation and community cohesion seems so battered, we need to anticipate the challenge from our children.

And we have to hope that we can answer, with reasonable honesty and historic accuracy, that we tried to know what was right and to act on it.

THE PRESS

From
Spiro
Agnew
to
the JOA

CHAPTER
SIX

J.N. Heiskell: A giant of journalism

When the 101st Airborne troops rumbled into Little Rock, Ark., in 1957 to enforce federal court-ordered school desegregation, the reaction of the populace was almost unanimous.

Almost, but not quite. Although the people of Arkansas condemned President Dwight Eisenhower roundly for his insistence that federal court orders are the law of the land, the state's largest newspaper, the Arkansas Gazette, supported President Eisenhower and denounced the state's governor, Orval Faubus, who had mounted the barricades against federal authority.

For its stand, the Gazette absorbed abuse and loss of circulation. But it also did something important. In the words of the late A.J. Liebling, "it confirmed the golden legend of a free and fearless press."

The man who permitted that stand to be made died in Little Rock last week at the age of 100. John Netherland Heiskell, one of the real giants of American journalism and for 70 years the editor of the Gazette, had been true to his sense of symmetry to the end, rounding life out to an even century.

JAN. 1, 1973

When the crunch came in Little Rock, when that small Southern capital became an international symbol of bigotry and hypocrisy, J.N. Heiskell did not blink or ask his editors to fall back.

Mr. Heiskell went to the office every day, including Saturday and Sunday, until his 99th birthday. He dictated editorials over the phone after that.

Mr. Liebling said of the Gazette in the Little Rock school crisis: "The Gazette held with law and order — recognition of the validity of the 14th Amendment as interpreted by the Supreme Court — while the Democrat, the other paper, took up for peace and harmony, which is not the same thing when the going gets rough."

The gentle, frail Mr. Heiskell — then 85 and 20 years past the retirement that normal men accept — was the real hero of that episode. For he was a Southern patrician, born in the decade after the Civil War, steeped in regional history and habits, a man who loved his state and city. He was also a man who faced unhappy advertisers and a conservative business community across the luncheon table — and yet stayed steadfast in support of his rambunctious editors.

It must have been harder for him, far harder, than for the generation of Southern editors born in the 20th Century. He, perhaps more than they, recognized the peculiarities of the South and its resistance to change. Yet when the crunch came in Little Rock, when that small Southern capital became an international symbol of bigotry and hypocrisy, J.N. Heiskell did not blink or ask his editors to fall back.

Even when a well-organized boycott cost the Gazette fully 10 percent of its circulation and more, the Old Man and the Old Red Bitch — as the Gazette, the oldest newspaper west of the Mississippi, was once called by an early 20th Century governor — did not back down.

Why? In 1958, accepting an award for the Gazette's performance on that episode, Mr. Heiskell tried to explain: "Every newspaper must come to judgment and accounting for the course that forms its image and its character. It is to be more than a mechanical recorder of news; if it is to be a moral and intellectual institution rather than an industry or a property, it must fulfill the measure of its obligation, even though, in the words of St. Paul, it has to endure affliction. It must have a creed and a mission. It must have dedication. It must fight the good fight. Above all else it must keep the faith."

In a cynical age, his words may sound pompous and stilted. But life for J.N. Heiskell was real and earnest, and he spoke not just words and ideals but articles of faith.

My own memory of Mr. Heiskell comes from the period after the Little Rock crisis had passed its crest, after the Gazette had rallied the city's moderate leadership and gotten the public schools open again, after the boycott had ended and the subscribers had begun to come home. The courage of the Gazette and its blunt honesty had begun to reap their reward.

I remember him as the man of courage, but also as a crotchety grammarian who loved to debate the finer points of the language, a history buff whose memory embraced most of the life span of his state. He was a man who insisted on a scrupulous separation of the news and editorial functions of the newspaper, and a wit whose wry humor is legend among journalists.

Once, when a Gazette columnist had written something disparaging about a garden club beautification project, a formidable dowager type descended on Mr. Heiskell and berated him nonstop for several minutes. Finally, when he could interject a word, he took the lady and led her to the offending journalist.

This, he said to the writer, is Mrs. So-and-So from the garden club. Then, turning on his heels, he added, "And may God have mercy on your soul."

To his sports editor, Mr. Heiskell presented a special problem. He had little interest in sports and did not often read the sports pages. In fact, he told sports editor Orville Henry, he read the sports section only a day or so every year. "Your problem," he told Henry, "is to know which day."

The Gazette was and is consistently Democratic. Harry Ashmore, the executive editor of the Gazette during the days of the school crisis, supposedly asked about that in 1948, when he was new at the paper.

"Is it true," he is supposed to have asked Mr. Heiskell, "that the Gazette never bolted the Democratic Party?"

Without a word, Mr. Heiskell is supposed to have gone over to the door, looked up and down the hall to see whether anyone was nearby, and then closed the door against intruding ears.

Almost in a whisper, according to Gazette folklore, Mr. Heiskell said, "We went Whig twice."

Most of us thought the story was apocryphal. Later, however, we discovered that the Gazette had indeed lent its support to two Whig candidates during its early pre-Civil War history.

Today, in an era when newspapers have generally fled their partisan origins, the Gazette is still basically a Democratic paper. It did support Winthrop Rockefeller, who became the state's first Republican governor since Reconstruction Days and ended the long tenure of the Faubus regime.

But the incident, in any case, tells more about Mr. Heiskell's love of tradition than about his partisanship. For he was a gentle, courtly partisan whose larger concerns — a passion for truth and an abiding intellectual curiosity — were the overwhelming facets of his character.

The full impact of his long tenure at the Gazette hit me one day in the early '60s when the Arkansas Legislature was at long last considering repeal of the state's old law banning the teaching of evolution in the schools. The statute — one of the last of the so-called monkey laws passed during the era of the Scopes trial — had been on the books since the 1920s.

Researching the history of the statute, I discovered that it had been enacted in a public referendum after a long and bitter fight over religious dogmas. Leading the fight against its enactment was a blue-ribbon committee composed of university and college presidents and other prominent citizens. One of them was J.N. Heiskell, editor of the Arkansas Gazette.

During 70 years as the boss of a newspaper, a man is bound to get in a great many fights.

It is the measure of John Netherland Heiskell's character and courage that he lived long enough to see his judgment vindicated in so many of them.

(Joe Stroud was an editorial writer on the Arkansas Gazette in the early 1960s.)

Press must be free to criticize officials

Seldom has the press been confronted with problems of fairness that were more subtle and more complex than those raised this year by the Watergate and Agnew episodes.

Seldom, too, have politicians tried harder than they are now to stretch perfectly reasonable legal doctrines to protect themselves and their colleagues against fair comment and searching press criticism.

President Richard Nixon has urged that Vice President Spiro Agnew be granted the "presumption of innocence." He and other public officials have complained that the Watergate abuses have resulted in "trials in the press." Our mail at the Free Press suggests that the public is inclined to share that attitude to at least some degree.

If it is still possible, though, I would like to try to persuade readers to think through the politicians' argument before accepting it as the whole truth.

My impression is that the presumption of innocence is a legal doctrine, designed to protect the accused in criminal proceedings. It means that, no matter what seems to be the case, the individual must be shown to be guilty of a crime before he can be punished.

SEPT. 27, 1973

The presumption of innocence was never intended to protect a public official from criticism, from the effects of investigative reporting, or from the exposure of untoward facts about him or her.

The doctrine does not mean that fingers cannot be pointed or accusations made before a trial. A trial starts with a pretrial accusation: from a witness, from the press, from a grand jury, from a prosecutor, from the police.

Moreover, once evidence is produced — as apparently it is about to be in the Agnew case and as it has been in the Watergate case — the situation changes. A judge can decide there is "probable cause" to believe a crime has been committed and the individual in question was a party to it.

Evidence can be presented, obviously, in advance of a conviction. The individual comes under a cloud. He may suffer adverse consequences to his business, his profession, or his reputation.

The presumption of his innocence protects him from conviction without trial, but it may not spare him all the consequences of being accused on the basis of evidence. All of this is true even when the individual involved is a private citizen. And if he is an important enough private citizen, the damaging accusations will be in the newspapers.

If, however, he is a public official, the rules are far less in his favor. Certainly the presumption of innocence was never intended to protect a public official from criticism, from the effects of investigative reporting, or from the exposure of untoward facts about him or her.

The U.S. Supreme Court has recognized that the press need not treat public officials with the same circumspection that applies to private citizens. The First Amendment guarantee is based on the idea that the press must be free to write critical stories about public officials if we are to be a free society. This doctrine permits us considerably more latitude in dealing with public servants.

Even in libel law, the Supreme Court has recognized that the press must be free to report and to question the actions of public officials without the same risk of libel that would be involved in dealing with a private citizen. The landmark Supreme Court case, New York Times vs. Sullivan, made that distinction clear, and the court's doctrine has since been expanded.

The reason is that a public official does not hold office as a matter of right. He holds office because the people or the people's representatives have entrusted him with office. They give, and they can take away.

Moreover, they can hold him to a higher standard of accountability than the criminal laws do. At least at the next election, they can remove a man from office because they don't like his reputation or because they don't like the silly grin on his face or whatever. In some instances, they are able to recall a public official with no explanation at all.

In the case of a president or vice president of the United States, the machinery for taking away the people's gift of office is more cumbersome, but it is there all the same.

Every aspect of a public official's conduct in office is subject to scrutiny. It has to be that way. Though newspapers ought to be prudent and responsible in reporting the facts about such dealings, they must report the truth as best they can.

Throughout both the Watergate and Agnew episodes, the press has not been far off base on the main particulars of the stories. We have had to deal too often with rumors and leaks, but the record shows that the press has been engaged generally in revealing truth rather than circulating rumors.

Even the partisans of this administration must surely acknowledge that, in many of the instances now pursued to culmination, there was fire beneath all that smoke. The press has served to expose wrongdoing and to force the politicians to try to deal with it.

Thus, Vice President Agnew now operates under a cloud because the press has reported unfolding facts, such as the investigation by the Maryland prosecutor and the U.S. Department of Justice. Not many people I know in the media are interested in railroading the vice president to jail; indeed, many of us feel a surge of sympathy for him in his troubles.

But if we are obliged to grant Spiro Agnew the presumption of innocence so far as conviction on possible criminal charges is concerned, we are duty-bound to pursue the story of his troubles and of his possible misdeeds with all the vigor at our command.

The politician accepts the risk of public criticism and scrutiny. It is a part of holding office.

It was a politician rather than a newsman who described best the role of the politician and the risk he takes.

As Harry Truman put it, "If you can't stand the heat, get out of the kitchen."

'Mr. Knight': A mentor, critic and friend

For those of us who were his editors, it was, quite literally, a death in the family.

John S. Knight, who was buried Saturday in his beloved Akron, was more than just "the boss." He was friend, teacher, tormentor, critic and protector.

Free Press readers, or at least most of them, remember his "Editor's Notebook," which appeared in this space for so many years. He was a very public man — laying his personal credibility on the line every week in an open, conversational way that told much about him as well as much about public affairs. So many people felt they knew Jack Knight.

JUNE 21, 1981

John S. Knight was a curmudgeon. He loved to banter with people and challenge them. At a party he would hold court. The topic of the conversation would vary, but the manner of the encounter left an indelible impression, especially if he chose you for his foil.

His columns tended to show that side of him: blunt, sometimes acid, clear, unpredictable. They also reflected his love of sports, especially horse racing,

Mr. Knight's relationship to his editors was based on an almost passionate insistence on their independence. He might disagree with you openly and vocally, but what most angered him was timidity.

and his passion for politics. He loved to write from personal encounters with public people and from being present at events. This was no ivory-tower editor.

One of the crusades that preoccupied Mr. Knight in his later years was opposition to the Vietnam War. He hated war and especially that war, and he was an early and persistent critic of American involvement in Vietnam. I found it impressive that his mind was so open to dissent, his views so fresh and strong, right to the end of his 86 years. Even last month, in his final visit to Detroit, he was strong of voice and view.

There was another side to Mr. Knight that always surprised me and would undoubtedly amaze even regular readers. It was a gentle, sentimental side.

One lovely day, about 10 years ago, I went from Detroit to Akron to talk to Jack Knight about an editorship. The option then was the job of editor of the editorial page at the Akron Beacon Journal (I was appointed to that job, and it was announced, but a chain of events kept me in Detroit).

The lunch with Mr. Knight was a part of the hiring process there that I dreaded. He awed me, especially then. I expected a grilling.

There was indeed some of that; there always was. But the larger part of the discussion was an almost lyrical description by him of his town — of Akron — and of what it meant to him. He loved that community in a special and a paternal way. He talked about its warts as well as its good attributes, but always with love. I had not anticipated such a gentle and sentimental soliloquy. But over the years, many of his notes to me about my columns were in response to sentimental pieces about human situations. When I wrote a column about the death of a friend, Mr. Knight wrote back a brief note saying he had found it "moving."

He liked pieces about the city and its life, but the warmest praise came in response to those to which you would least expect him to react: about a walk with a dog, or about the end of summer, or about taking a daughter to college.

Mr. Knight's relationship to his editors was based on an almost passionate insistence on their independence. He might disagree with you openly and vocally, but what most angered him was timidity. He did not want us looking over our shoulders to see whether someone was watching our every opinion from on high. Yet you knew he cared about quality.

His was a high standard, and I remain in awe of the tradition he built.

He encouraged an informality; he expected us to call him "Jack." I never could. He was my friend, but he always remained "Mr. Knight" to me.

It was not from fear or a sense of distance or even because of the difference in our ages.

Some people earn a right to respect and deference. John Knight had surely earned that much with me. He was a remarkable mentor and friend.

And I think he would not mind my writing, again, about the death of a friend.

Life through Lou Cook's eyes is a joy

When I first began to work with Louis Cook on the Free Press editorial page — almost 16 years ago now — I quickly decided that the accurate way to describe him was as "the only 6-foot-4 elf in captivity."

Lou Cook is also a master at what is now almost a lost art in American journalism: the short reporting piece that can evoke a mood and tell a story with almost no unnecessary words and with a compelling grace and charm.

When he came in a few days ago to tell me that he had decided to retire — with a suddenness and a disdain for the ordinary niceties such things usually elicit — it was an emotional scene for both of us. As a writer, he has had a special role here at the Free Press. His reports have given character and a sense of place to the paper for more than three decades. But Lou Cook has also been, among my coworkers, virtually my best friend.

For years after I came to Detroit, and for some years after I became editor, I would go to lunch with Lou whenever I had no obligations for, as he called my outside obligations, "some affair of state." He has always insisted on having one favorite restaurant. The old Mayfield Bar & Grill, with paneled walls and an indulgent chef, was his favorite for many years.

MARCH 23, 1984

Life for Lou Cook has been and is a sort of magic unfolding. I have seen him stand in the middle of a virtually destroyed section of the city and find beauty and hope in it.

He and I had a Friday ritual there: finnan haddie. We tried our best to be there on Fridays. If you were "Mr. Cook's friend," the chef, Walter, would bring out some little special sidelight — a paté, perhaps, or a special salad dressing. It was years before I ever became anything more than "Mr. Cook's friend."

Then one Friday I looked up at Lou, and he looked at me, and we recognized a truth that the ritual had concealed: Neither of us liked finnan haddie. I haven't had it since.

That is the way life has been and is with Lou Cook. It is easy in his company to see the world as a more benign place than it often seems to be for others. Though he has had more than his share of personal grief, including especially the recent death of his wife Frances, he has seemed to move through life with a special immunity to the discouragements ordinary mortals face.

Life for Lou Cook has been and is a sort of magic unfolding. For years he lived a bachelor's life, renting small places in various parts of the city. He would amble through parts of the city, stopping to help strangers or to inspect a flower in a crannied wall, with an enthusiasm that sometimes belied the reality. I have seen him stand in the middle of a virtually destroyed section of the city and find beauty and hope in it.

His reporting technique involves describing in loving detail the filigree on a building or the gentle ironies of some human situation. I remember fragments of his pieces, such as his description of his childhood as "the time when Dad was young and Mom was pretty."

In that format, he has few, if any, peers. He has done so many things, studied so many areas, that one is tempted to call him a Renaissance man. He worked on a farm, and he can recall with incredible precision every detail of every tool he ever used. He studied mathematics and physics, and he will occasionally toss off a random piece of information that will confound you.

He won a Bronze Star, and he won it the hard way — as a sergeant who single-handedly captured a dozen or so German soldiers after staring them down in a European forest confrontation. He was and is a solid union man.

Lou played basketball and studied the classics at Drake University and later went to the University of Iowa and to the University of Chicago. His head, which has sometimes seemed to me to refuse to deal with the realities that others see, is full of allusions to Greek and Roman mythology.

You push the wrong button and Lou will burst into song, with a beautifully resonant baritone, or will unleash a string of poetry he memorized when, as he puts it, he was "a callow youth." On dark days, I have occasionally quoted back at him what I could remember of Matthew Arnold's "Dover Beach." He didn't like — doesn't like — the part about our being here "as on a darkling plain ..., where ignorant armies clash by night."

His world does not consist of "darkling plains." It is a kaleidoscope, full of variety and charm that transcend pain and tragedy. We have had obscure and perverse arguments about whether life is basically sad or basically happy. Lou believes it is "a great adventure." I believe, with Tolstoy, that we have to understand it is sad before we can be happy.

The difference is probably more semantic than real. Even esoteric argument can be beautiful when it is a part of friendship.

This newspaper and its readers will miss Lou Cook and those loving little cameo shots of his world.

I will miss seeing his columns. But I will miss far more seeing my old friend every day. Such colleagues are rare. Such friends are even more precious.

Challenge is renewed to serve community

For more than 16 years, I have been in this spot almost every Sunday.

Except for a few extended trips abroad and a rare vacation break, I haven't missed a turn. Even on vacation or at a meeting, I have usually chosen to tap out the column on a little portable terminal and shoot the column back into the big computer system here at the Free Press.

The continuity might or might not matter to readers. It has mattered to me. When I went to Arkansas in 1974 to bury my father, and Richard Nixon chose that week to resign, I wrote about the way the two events — the personal and the national — were interrelated. I have this compulsion to try to connect what is going on with me with what is going on with the larger world.

Most of us, I think, are trying to do that. What does it mean to me that Eastern Europe is aflame with the passion of democratization? What does it mean to me that the community is hurting? What are our community

Nov. 26, 1989

It is up to us to show that we do care about the community, that we have something to say to the community, that we deserve to be a part of your lives.

values, our hopes, our fears, and how do they fit or clash with my own values, hopes and fears? How can I as an individual try to help shape the community? Indeed, in a big, brawling industrial city, what is community?

To have this forum has been and is a very special privilege. I have had as much freedom and as much autonomy as any other editor in America, I suspect. That is an extraordinary gift to a kid from Arkansas who used to seek solitude in the top of the hay barn just to play around with words and ideas. I count myself lucky to have had such a forum for a single day. To have it threatened, as it was during the long controversy over the joint operating agreement, was a special agony. Was I destined to lose this forum? Was the Free Press going to lose its place in the life of this community? I found it a paralyzing prospect.

I hope, though, those fears did not show through too much. We have tried to continue to do our job day after day, without surrendering to the uncertainty. For the most part, I think that we did, that we spoke honestly and forthrightly about the life of the community, that we spoke out with intensity about such things as the state of the schools and the future of the city and the curse of injustice. I am proud of my colleagues and of the Free Press.

Now, this week, we will begin an important transition in the history of our relationship to the community. The long JOA process has plainly done some damage. Some are skeptical; many do not understand what will be happening, though we have described it to the point of being a bore.

It is up to us to demonstrate that we will preserve the qualities you have prized about your Free Press and that we will keep trying to improve on the things that frustrate you. It is up to us to show that we do care about the community, that we have something to say to the community, that we deserve to be a part of your lives.

I am truly thankful now that this is a transition column and not a final column. We've been given a new chance to try, every day, to get better at our jobs than we were yesterday. That's a splendid opportunity, but it is only an opportunity. There are no guarantees.

So we'll begin tomorrow to try to make this new arrangement work for ourselves and for you. There will be some losses, I'm sure, and certainly some suspicions. The JOA will be cited again and again to explain things with which it has no connection. I believe there will also be some gains, not just for us but for the readers.

The most important gain, I hope, is that there will continue to be separate, independent voices arguing about the future of the community and about how best to strengthen the community's prospects. In an imperfect world, what we have is a framework that lets us continue to try to play that role.

In the end, you will have to decide whether we do so in a way that is more often right than wrong. I hope you will be reassured by what you see. I am glad that we will have the chance to go on being a part of your lives.

FAMILY

From Mom on the Farm to Children in the City

Good-bye to a home

It was her last night in the old house, and she called, she said, "because I just had to talk to someone tonight."

For roughly 40 years they had called it home, but now Dad was sick and she was tired, and they were moving to a house in town. The old house is being rented out, along with the farm, because it will be easier for them to cope with life in the town, among friends.

So there she was, alone in the house with the ghosts, remembering. There was a continuity about life there, a sense of stability and of place that fewer and fewer Americans know.

My father had helped build the original four rooms with his own hands. This addition marked the coming of a brother. That one came when three sons became too much for two bedrooms. A third wing marked their growing prosperity and Mother's realization of her dream of a real kitchen.

Central air-conditioning and brick veneer had brought a measure of comfort to the little frame building, and it had the look of well-ordered farm life about it.

OCT. 6, 1971

So it is good-bye to the old house. Good-bye to the trees I saw planted and where last summer I built a swing for my youngest. Good-bye to the honeysuckle by the road and to the barn where 4-H projects were carried out.

Forty years in one house is a long time. The 100 years that my father's family has lived on that land is even longer. My father remembers lying in bed at night, in the old house that was my grandfather's headquarters, listening to the wolves at the edge of the woods.

Improvements came slowly to the Arkansas farm country during my childhood. Electrical power came only at the end of World War II, and then after a protracted struggle. The paved highway to town represented a major political breakthrough in the early '50s. Congressmen were judged by their success at pushing the Corps of Engineers to control floods.

The gravel on the country road that ran past the house was — would you believe it? — war surplus, taken up off the grid of roads that served the "relocation center," which is what the government called the place where the Japanese Americans were interned during the war.

In winter, the old road was sometimes impassable, turned to mud by the tender care the county judge's road crew provided. In summer, the dust was deep, searing to bare feet in the sun, cool and reassuring in the shade. Mercifully, there was shade, though there were also thorns.

My father had always celebrated the country life. The town, he thought (then, population 3,000), diluted parental control. Town boys turned soft from inactivity. Better to tend cows and keep chickens and mend fences and eat fresh vegetables. Ah, the hazards that lie in the city.

It was and is, for at least a few, a good life. More and more, though, even the remaining farm folk are moving into town, huddling together for schools, for security and, mostly, for the human fellowship. The farm communities are almost literally disappearing, with mechanization and consolidation of farms.

My mother remembers a time when there were 17 families on that one farm. I can remember seven. Now there is one.

The community is larger and looser. The school is consolidated. The people have scattered off the land, and those who remain do not celebrate the country life in the same way.

It was Detroit, of course, that did all that. Mr. Ford's revolution started the changing of the country life. The same road that made it easier to get home from town made it easier to get from home to someplace else.

Moreover, the mechanization of the farm also had its effect. I remember the night Grandfather's barn burned. It was a spectacular, eerie scene, something out of a Southern gothic novel. A lot of the horses were lost, and it hastened the process of coming to terms with mechanization. There was never again a big collection of mules and horses on the place. As the tractors came, people left.

Something was lost, but those who knew the old life will tell you much was gained. They did not relish the hot, still nights with no electric fans, or the relentless mosquitoes, or the muddy roads, or the endless cotton rows. Machines meant liberation.

Not for all, of course. For some machines meant exile and life in the cities and the frustrating attempt to adapt to different patterns.

For all, though, life is changed. More than ever, life is flux.

So it is good-bye to the old house. Good-bye to the trees I saw planted and where last summer I built a swing for my youngest. Good-bye to the honeysuckle by the road and to the barn where 4-H projects were carried out.

Times change, and needs change, and even home has to change.

But one thing more, though, Mother. I only hope you remembered to check the attic.

There's this box of old love letters …

A bittersweet tale of flowers and frost

She is 17, and she loves the flowers.

She loves them in the spring in flats at Eastern Market and through the summer days.

So Saturday night, when the word of a frost warning came, she took all the papers and plastic bags and pots she could find, and she began to cover them.

Finally, she came by our room, as though to say good night.

"What's wrong?" her mother asked.

"There are so many of them," she said, "and they are so pretty, and they're going to die. I couldn't find enough papers."

"Maybe the frost won't be that heavy this time," we offered.

"I hate to see them die so soon."

"To everything there is a season," her mother said, more to herself than to her daughter, "a time to live and a time to die."

So at midnight we put on our robes, and we found more paper and made a coverlet for the impatiens. The chill of fall was in the air.

SEPT. 16, 1975

It was a sad, sweet moment, this night of the frost warning. A sense of change and yet a shared sense of community.

The tears came down her cheeks as we covered them and then the marigolds and geraniums.

"I didn't think it would frost so soon," she said again.

"It is early," I told her, "but remember there's beauty in all the seasons."

"Thank you, Daddy," she said as we finished up. It was warm enough to cut through the chill night. She was "my little rosebud" again, and not a grown-up touch-me-not.

I looked up the passage from Ecclesiastes and handed it to her. "A time to plant and a time to uproot." The New English Bible has lost some of the music, but the thought is there.

"Someone made it into a song," she said.

And then she went up to bed.

It was a sad, sweet moment, this night of the frost warning. A sense of change and yet a shared sense of community.

I don't know why I even recount it. It contributes little or nothing, I suppose, to keeping the city together, or bringing enlightenment to any of the world's problems. No one else, I suspect, even cares.

Yet I have a recurring feeling that much of what we in the media write and talk about as important really isn't, and that we seldom talk about much of what matters most.

Our concerns tend to be so esoteric and programmatic; we have to keep reminding ourselves that societies and governments exist for people, instead of vice versa.

And we have to remind ourselves what matters most.

What matters most? I never know for sure anymore.

Sometimes, though, at midnight on a chilly night, I think maybe I know a little:

A young girl who tries to create a little beauty, who knows the flowers' names and who rejoices at spring and weeps at frost. A moment shared between parent and child. A sense of the seasons. The last tomato and the first red leaf on the maple. The stillness of midnight, and the splendor of the stars.

Those may not be the beginning and the end of life, and in a city troubled by unemployment and other ills, it may be almost ignoble to fasten on frostbitten plants rather than suffering people.

Still, I'm glad she cared and glad she routed me from my bed to try to stave off for one day more the killing frost.

As she says, "They are so pretty."

The world can find lessons in Dr. Seuss

One of the joys of having a child is that you have a good excuse to read the Dr. Seuss books.

And one of the pains of seeing your youngest grow up is that she no longer crawls on your lap and asks you to read "Yertle the Turtle" or "On Beyond Zebra!"

Dr. Seuss is a splendid social commentator who disguises himself as a children's author. He makes the bedtime story fun for parents, and as an added bonus, the kids even like him.

"Yertle the Turtle," for instance, is one of my favorites. Yertle the Turtle aspired to be the king of the pond, of all he surveyed. He insisted that all the turtles stack themselves up, one on top of the other, letting him build a kind of turtle Tower of Babel, with himself up on top. He kept demanding that the pile of turtles on which he rested be stacked higher and higher.

JAN. 18, 1976

Now, sadly, my youngest does not so often read Dr. Seuss anymore. Before long, I fear, even I will have to stop.

Finally, down at the bottom of the stack, a little turtle named Mack burped, and the whole stack came tumbling down.

In the immortal words of Dr. Seuss:

And today the great Yertle, that Marvelous he,
Is King of the Mud. That is all he can see.
And the turtles, of course ... all the turtles are free
As turtles and, maybe, all creatures should be.

For a moral, you have to admit, it beats the devil out of "Cinderella" or "Little Red Riding Hood."

Another of the Dr. Seuss stories that often comes in handy is "On Beyond Zebra!" about a little boy who decides he knows it all because he has learned the alphabet that ends with "z is for zebra." So he is introduced to all the wonderful letters that lie beyond.

Unfortunately, even the otherworldly new electronic gadgets we now use to set type on the editorial page can't reproduce those new letters. And our art department, I fear, has never gone "beyond zebra."

My favorite is the Um, which is for Umbus, which Dr. Seuss tells us is:

A sort of a Cow, with one head and one tail,
But to milk this great cow you need more than one pail!
She has ninety-eight faucets that give milk quite nicely.
Perhaps ninety-nine. I forget just precisely.
And, boy! She is something most people don't see
Because most people stop at the Z, but not me!

There are other marvelous creatures in the world "On Beyond Zebra!" I agree with Dr. Seuss' young hero, who has the marvelous name of Conrad Cornelius o'Donald o'Dell:

"This is really great stuff!
"And I guess the old alphabet
"ISN'T enough!"

Sometimes, as I reflect on the contrast between the somnolent '50s, when I was in college, and the turbulence of the period since the mid-'60s, I feel we have been moving through that strange land "beyond zebra." The times have baffled and mystified us.

For many people, of course, this has been terrifying. The times have seemed out of joint.

I must say these times have sometimes terrified me. And what have terrified me most have been the snake-oil salesmen and charlatans who have offered us simplistic answers to our problems during this remarkable period.

If we can get our heads together, though, and see what is really happening, maybe it will be less terrifying. Our society has been disorderly and disjointed, contentious and troubled, true.

But why? Because the feudal structure by which blacks were once kept "in their place" has been shattered. Because mobility and ease of communication have enlarged both our immediate world and its dangers. Because we have been forced by events to face the wastefulness of our society. Because we are coming squarely up against the inadequacy of some of our institutions. Because people are no longer willing to go like sheep to the slaughter to the wars their leaders make for them.

Of course it is dangerous with many of the elements of the old order gone. I almost wrote, "gone with the wind." Of course it is worrisome.

Maybe that is why so many people prefer to stick with the world that ends with "z is for zebra" — the established rote, the reflexive answer, the dreary longing for a day long lost.

Somehow, though, even on this uneasy and strange course charted only in a fantasy book for children, there seem to be adventure, and challenge, and life worth the hazards.

But then, being the father of a recently small girl, I have read Dr. Seuss as well as "Dr. Strangelove," "Yertle the Turtle" as well as the murder of Yablonski. I find it hard to try to reject that world "beyond zebra."

Now, sadly, my youngest does not so often read Dr. Seuss anymore.

Before long, I fear, even I will have to stop.

What a pity, though! A is for Ape and B is for Bear may be more orderly, and they may be what we're all pulling back to.

But I must say I've been glad to have been alive during this time when we've been feeling our way "beyond zebra."

Even big cities need Aunt Gertrudes

Aunt Gertrude won't be giving piano lessons anymore.

For almost as many years as I can remember, she has been teaching willing and reluctant little fingers what to do on the keyboard. Well past normal retirement time, she had stayed at it, remaining a part of the community, being younger herself for her contact with the young.

The young have been a part of her life for many years. Some of my earliest memories are of the kindergarten she ran in her home before the war and of the piano lessons.

Her husband, now gone these good many years, was a town institution, too — first coach, then principal, then superintendent, then postmaster, finally also president of the school board.

But Aunt Gertrude has always been my favorite. My father's only sister, she is as gregarious as he was taciturn. She has sung in the choir at the Methodist Church, too.

This fall, though, the accumulated weight of a series of family tragedies finally forced her to run a little note in the town paper that she was not going to be giving lessons anymore. She had been phasing out her pupils anyhow, but the death of a young grandson and the critical illness of one of her daughters have now brought it to an end.

My point is that in communities, whether big, rough industrial towns or little farming and railroad towns, it is the Aunt Gertrudes of this world who

AUG. 28, 1977

Even big cities need people who care about people, who somehow convey the point that there is in human society something ultimately redeeming and valiant and hopeful.

determine whether community exists, whether life has any redeeming quality, whether the young are subjected to any of the gentling influences of civilization. People.

People have an enormous capacity to adapt to forces that may threaten to break or to destroy institutions.

I remember from the days before the civil rights revolution touched our little town that Aunt Gertrude had the same fears as anyone else about what change would mean.

But I remember, too, in recent years asking her about how things were going in the public schools there, with which she maintained a tangential and informal connection. "We're getting along fine," she would say.

Her ability to adapt, after almost a lifetime of living under the social code of the Old South, struck me as remarkable at the time. Again, though, people adapt.

In the period of the great urban riots, the country — and particularly journalists — cast about for answers to what was happening in the cities and the country. We searched for, and for a while expected to find, grandiose solutions to the sweeping problems of urban society.

I do not mean to suggest that what we need to save the cities is a lot of urban versions of my Aunt Gertrude. In big cities, institutions take on more importance, and individuals seem to count for less.

When there is a garbage strike, we can try to remove our garbage somewhere rather than let it rot in the garage, but it isn't easy. When the schools don't function right, we can go to school board meetings and complain or even move our children to private schools, but it is likely to have only a small impact on the whole.

And the cities do urgently need substantial amounts of public and private investment if they are to find the new economic base that is to replace the old one that has decayed.

One thing, though, I think I have learned about cities in the past 10 years. The solutions, while more difficult than we expected, are also in some ways simpler and less high-blown than we thought. People do not escape the urban ghetto en masse; they do it one at a time.

And even big cities, if they are ever to become communities, need Aunt Gertrudes: They need people who care about people, who teach little fingers about Chopin and Mozart, and who somehow convey the point that there is in human society something ultimately redeeming and valiant and hopeful.

They are teachers who bother to teach, policemen who see the old lady on the corner as a human being and not just a chronic caller about imagined horrors. They are people who see, beneath skin color, a common humanity.

And if we are to build a city, we have to understand what they mean and how they and we have to build that sense of community and of the importance of individuals.

In the end, if we save the cities, it will not be because there has been a Marshall Plan for cities, though we may need that, too. It will be because we — and the Aunt Gertrudes of this world — have put forth a cumulative effort that adds up, at last and once again, to a community worthy of the name.

A father's hopes are worth remembering

He was a tough old man, my father was, but in the autumn he mellowed, like the corn.

He was a farmer at heart, though for many years he worked at something else, and what he really wanted me to be was a farmer, too.

For years I worked on my 4-H projects, which came to fruition on crisp autumn days under big tents that smelled of hay and cow manure. It was a good time for him, standing by, kibitzing with the farmers from the far corners of the county, talking livestock, talking crops.

At such a time, in such a setting, he became a different man — animated, passionate, warm. He was consumed, too, by his interest in what I was doing.

I did it all with enough diligence — there are scrapbooks full of faded ribbons in the top of the closet and the bottom of the desk — but my heart was often in other things: football, the newspaper downtown, the poetry I committed to memory and recited with my school-teacher mother, politics. And though I enjoyed those times with him — it was a common ground — I could never love the rhythm of the earth and the mystery of things that grow in it and on it the way he did.

OCT. 1, 1978

When I think of those times, I think of new jackets and old blue jeans, of how much we want for our children, and how seldom they are able to give it to us.

My Lord, how he loved it! He could see things on a plant or in a herd of cows I could not see. He could sense a commotion in the upper pasture three-quarters of a mile away. He fretted over every strand of wire on every row of fence we had.

I did not dislike it, but I could not share the full passion he had for it.

Still, there is a time every year, when the mornings first get an edge to them and the moon becomes full like a harvest, when I think of him and how he cared about the farm and farming people. I remember the sense of becoming a man in his eyes, riding with him and his friend to the fair.

He was proud to be a father then, prouder than at any other time. Though he wasn't a man of many words, he would grow more talkative in those times, talking of things that only partly possessed me, but talking nonetheless, granting acceptance, even laughing a bit.

I remember a long trip to the state capital one year, in a pickup truck a hundred miles over bad roads, man to man, companions in a golden October adventure.

And when I think of those times, I think of new jackets and old blue jeans, of how much we want for our children, and how seldom they are able to give it to us. I think of his wanting me to be a farmer, and my trying, and my not caring enough.

I think, too, of my own children, of the two home recently for a weekend break from the new college routine. Of sitting with my son, watching football, saying to him I was glad to have him home and, forgetting, saying it again. Of my hopes for them and their frustrations with me. Of how so much of what seems to matter so much matters so little, and how the small human bonds really matter.

None of this matters a whit to any but me, I know. There is so much on our agenda. I should be trying to deal this Sunday morning not with a remembrance of my dead father but with the ungodly long agenda all the special interests have put before us on the November ballot. Or the city, or public affairs, or the cynicism that so many of us feel.

Still, every fall there comes a day when the temperature and humidity are just right, where the sun rises soft and radiant, where the underglow on the trees shows through, when I think of that time and place, and of him.

And I regret that I couldn't give him what he so earnestly wanted: for me to care about that place and that process as much as he did.

He understood, finally, that I had to do what I had to do, and in the end he accepted my choice, and my inability to accept his preference. I would go back in the fall, and he would show me the crops and the cows, and I would be interested and make all the sage observations about the growing things I could remember.

I always left wishing I cared as much as he did.

I still do.

With gentle hands, she shaped young lives

You cannot have known Miss Marybelle McQuistion, so why should I think it would matter to you that she died this week in a small Arkansas town, at the age of 93?

But for almost all of us, whether raised in the South, the Midwest or on the northwest side of Detroit, there is or was a Miss Marybelle.

She was what would have been described, in the Victorian language applied to such matters in years gone by, as a maiden lady schoolteacher. No one in town knew how old she was until the day she died.

When I first encountered her, as a gentle, gray-haired first-grade teacher in the McGehee Grade School — she must have been 57 then — she was a source of comfort and reassurance in what was often for me a terrifying place.

Miss Marybelle's classroom was the first on the left, inside the front door of the old red-brick grammar school, even before you got to the office.

I went to the school just at the beginning of The War. I was born in 1936, in the hottest, driest summer of the Depression, and I entered school just after the start of The War.

MARCH 16, 1980

Miss Marybelle always seemed to suggest lilac water and gentle dedication. Somehow she took the formless clay my parents brought her, and she taught me to read and to begin to spell.

They were not good or happy times. We were not as poor as many, but we lived in a house on my grandfather's farm, and there were not many who did not have to scrap for everything.

It strikes many strange today to know that one 43 years old could have lived in a world without electricity or telephones until late in his grammar school years. The power lines had not been strung the eight miles out into the country where we lived.

In town, there was electrical power, and there were telephones, and there was arrogance. Out in the country, the struggle was to get the work done and to keep us disease-free and clean. In town, they had time for fripperies such as the movie theater and sports and the quiet pleasures of a small-town childhood.

So when I came to that first-grade world, without benefit of kindergarten, the old grade school seemed to me a place of daily terrors: indoor plumbing, electric clocks, children who were brasher than I, air-raid drills that spoke of destruction coming out of the sky, a routine that demanded a socialization I had not learned in my preschool years on the farm.

There were two first-grade teachers — and they each taught us half the day. Miss Marybelle taught reading-related subjects and art. Miss May Clayton taught arithmetic and other harsher disciplines. Miss Clayton was a distant cousin of mine, but she ruled her classroom with what seemed to my 6-year-old perceptions a harsh and unyielding hand.

Miss Marybelle always seemed, by contrast, to suggest lilac water and gentle dedication. Somehow she took the formless clay my parents brought her, and she taught me to read and to begin to spell. Phonics, painful science though it then seemed. The beginnings of a love for words.

Miss Marybelle also taught the 5-year-olds in the Methodist Sunday school, and it was she who made of me a Methodist. My mother had been a Baptist, and my father was a Methodist who was then not going to either church. My mother went off on a trip and left me to go to church with my cousin.

Her birthday was exactly a week before mine, and it happened to be her birthday. The heretic Methodists had a birthday party for her in Sunday school, with a cake and with the usual singing.

"The Baptists don't do this," I told Miss Marybelle.

"Come back next Sunday, and we'll have a party for you," she said.

That was the last the Baptists ever saw of me. It wasn't exactly St. Paul on the road to Damascus, but it sufficed for an early conversion, I suppose.

In later years, I was never totally sure Miss Marybelle could always keep straight which one of the Stroud boys I was. But I almost always saw her when I went back, and she appraised my children who came back with me with an eager eye and a sense of continuity. She was ever the gentle lady who had taught me how to read and who had helped me so much to make the world more manageable and less fear-invoking.

In my own children's experience — though it was not marked by the stability and continuity of growing up in and around a small and slow-changing town — there were Miss Marybelles, too, some of them in the Detroit schools: Miss Sibley, Miss Higgins, for instance.

Gentle people, who took lumps of clay and shaped them. Good teachers and school people, who understood the terrors of the innocent and dealt with them. They must have wondered at the modest rewards and the vicarious satisfactions. But they shaped our lives and gave us meaning.

That would not be a bad epitaph for Miss Marybelle or for any of us.

One of life's victims, she gave too much

She died by her own hand, there by her eggs in the cellar of the farmhouse.

There was no note, only a diary with no entries at all for the last few days before her death.

Many of her friends, even those who knew how she had been battered by life and abused by her husband, were surprised to learn that she had died, and how it had happened.

What they remembered about her was strength. Hers was the kind of quiet courage that her children will remember and cherish. She was what the priest or minister would call a good Christian woman — sacrificing for those around her, loving in the face of pain and unkindness directed at her, resourceful in giving to those around her. She was a victim in the classic dictionary sense, almost in a religious sense; she sacrificed so that others might live.

OCT. 4, 1981

Her suffering and pain inspired her children to struggle against the forces that make victims of the innocent.

Those who knew her best knew she gave too much — accepting what she could have resisted, bowing to what should not have been inevitable, unable to defend herself.

Her suffering and pain inspired her children to struggle against the forces that make victims of the innocent. I was never able to sense fully the searing nightmare that left her wounded and weary. I knew only that she was a good woman who deserved more for herself and couldn't ask for it and wasn't able to accept it when it was offered.

It is hard now, in an age of commercial farms and mechanical marvels, to appreciate fully how difficult her struggle for her own dignity and her children's dignity was.

At the farmers market in town, they called her the egg lady or the noodle lady. She eked out of her baking and her farm produce the money to rear four children. She shielded them as best she could from the abuse that was in the home, that came with drunken rage.

And when that difficult marriage entered its final phase — when her husband, after a stroke, could no longer practice his tyranny over her, she grieved for him. She tended him in his weakness as long as she could, though not as long as she meant to. More than most, she saw that he, too, was a victim.

Hers was an old-fashioned concept of duty — too old-fashioned for her own good. She tried to believe in the triumph of righteousness. She yearned for justice and accepted the teaching that the meek are blessed. But she did not inherit the Earth. She gave and gave and gave — so much so that in the end she could not fully accept the love that her children tried to give back to her.

I do not know that I can understand such patience in the face of suffering. My generation expects more and accepts less. If life deals us a bad hand, or if the cards that once seemed so full of promise turn against us, we want a new deal. And usually ask for it. Or demand it.

Which is better? I don't know. How much should we endure in patience and grace? There is redemptive suffering, and there are those whose sacrifice saves others. But there is pain that has too high a price. This is true victimization.

It's not the Earth the meek inherit, says one of the songs from "Camelot"; it's the dirt. And so, at times, it certainly seems.

She died in her work clothes. There seemed a bitter symbolism in that. So much struggle, so much long-suffering humility, so much pain. She died alone, too — "my kingdom is gone," her diary said. No golden slippers on her feet; only her work shoes, with the droppings from the henhouse stuck to the sole of one shoe. She was tired of keeping on keeping on, but she had gathered the eggs one last time. She had completed her chores.

I wish I knew whether her patience and her suffering were now being redeemed. I think there is an essential justice in the universe, some ultimate righting of wrongs, some squaring of accounts. I can't know or say just how, but life evens things out, I believe, in the end.

If there is a justice in the universe, if there is a Being of mercy and kindness and justice at the core of all existence, then without doubt she has some kind of peace. And if there is immortality, even only the immortality of keeping hope alive for those who come after, she must have achieved it.

And surely there is a place somewhere — a place beside still waters and amid green pastures — where she has found the peace she never quite knew on Earth.

Self-reliance? Mom wrote the book on it

To a son's question, "How're you doing?" her answer seldom varies.

"Busy," she will say. "I'm a little tired tonight. I worked all day at our hospital auxiliary's 'omelette day.' But we raised a lot of money."

By the end of the conversation, you may have wormed out of her that her trick knee has been acting up again, or there is a little growth on her face that worried the doctor. But it's okay.

In the meantime, she will have told you about what she's teaching her Sunday school class, who has died and who has gotten well, and how she's planning next year's project for her historical society.

In a world full of snarling self-pity and angry divisions, I find those conversations renewing and uplifting.

For almost 50 years of marriage, before he died in 1974, my father had sought to order her life as well as his around his specifications. Dinner was to be at 5:30 when he got home from work.

APRIL 4, 1982

She is not a feminist, at least not a conscious one, and yet in so many ways she has been what the argument over the role of women has been about.

He was proud and stubborn and exacting — too much of all those things — and she had devoted herself to him and his happiness with such faithfulness that I had wondered what would happen when he died.

It was a needless worry.

She plunged into self-sufficiency with such a will and an enthusiasm that I am awed.

When a neighbor — a young man she had taught in sixth grade — tried to encroach on the property line of the farm, she raised herself up to her full 5-foot-4, wagged her finger at him and said, "Now, Walter, you know better than that." He backed away, as he must have backed away when she demanded performance as he struggled with fractions or syntax years before.

When the town's Chamber of Commerce named her woman of the year and asked me to come back home and make the speech and present her award, she wept. So did I, for sheer pride in what she, unleashed after my dad's long illness, had done with her time and with what could have been her loneliness.

One night I called when the University of Arkansas' Razorbacks were playing a particularly good basketball game on television. "Did you see those Hawgs?" she wanted to know. I hadn't, but she gave me a five-minute soliloquy on the character and abilities of one of the stars. She liked him almost as much as Sidney Moncrief. She cares about "those boys."

She is not a feminist, at least not a conscious one, and yet in so many ways she has been what the argument over the role of women has been about. She protected and preserved her own identity. She struggled with the hardships of the Depression and the war years, making shirts of feed sacks, making sure her children stayed clean even when it meant pumping and heating water on the stove, fighting the frequent loneliness of the farm life.

Now in her seventies, she still conveys some of that young-girl naivete she must have had when she came, at 18, as a new bride down from the city to the hard life of the hot farm country. Don't believe it, though. She confronted cancer and beat it. She can take on the tax assessor or the lawyer or the young men at the bank, whom she probably taught, too. She can fend for herself.

There is no real reason you should care about this personal reflection. It is not even Mother's Day. There is no occasion, except that when I listened to her telling how she had just come back from a boat trip up the Mississippi, as a member of the governor's advisory commission on the tricentennial of the visit of LaSalle to Arkansas, it somehow seemed a remarkable thing.

Not because she is truly unique. Beneath the surface of the society, there are a multitude of such stories out there: people whose stubbornness and strength do not yield to adversity or discouragement and who somehow go through life triumphantly and untouched, people who touch us and our lives.

Still, in the larger perspective, she does matter to you. People matter, people who care, people who overcome.

In the midst of much that makes us brittle, there are some people who help make us strong.

The gum machine gave a lesson on life

What they faced, you might say, was the Moment of Truth at the Gum Ball Machine.

He, age 2½, was in charge of the pennies.

She, just under 18 months, stood by attentively, unable to work the lever but already very well schooled in what was at stake. In spite of the dentists and the pediatricians, they are born knowing about such things.

He had four pennies, scavenged up from Dad's pocket and Mom's purse.

First penny in. Out came a green gum ball (a little Chiclet, actually). Not bad. Not bad at all. Green was on everyone's Preferred Gum Ball List.

You could see the moment of indecision in his motion. The hand almost went to his mouth. But wait. He turned and handed that first, precious one to his waiting little sister. Somehow, an instinct for civility and fairness had prevailed over sibling rivalry.

As the second penny went in, Mom and Dad watched the drama played out. Black licorice. Ugh! He looked at Little Sister, already working on the green one. The cost of courtesy had just gone up. Crestfallen, he handed it to Mom.

FEB. 24, 1985

Big Brothers who remember to give the first piece of gum away aren't condemned, after all, always to accept licorice. Thanks be to the gods who watch over children who patronize gum ball machines.

The third penny. Black again. You could see panic starting to set in about the wages of generosity. Dad got this one.

Finally, penny No. 4. Bingo. A red piece. There was a sigh, a grin and a look almost of joy. This is a just universe. Big Brothers who remember to give the first piece of gum away aren't condemned, after all, always to accept licorice. Thanks be to the gods who watch over children who patronize gum ball machines.

In an era of assertiveness training and "Looking Out for No. 1," it was a sublime moment. He had risen above the natural impulse and been reinforced in his magnanimity. Score one for civility.

The incident was modest and personal, but the point is fundamental. It may be a tough world out there, but there is something to be said for trying to take the curse off it by showing a little human consideration.

It's odd how small lessons get deeply ingrained. I remember the lengths to which my mother went to teach me that if there are two pieces of chicken left on the platter, you don't take the best one for yourself. You leave it for your brother. I remember her dwelling on the message in the story of Solomon and the two women, each of whom claimed a child as her own. The real mother would be the first to revolt against the idea of cutting the child in half. There are relationships where looking out for No. 1 is not the guiding principle.

In less intimate human relationships, of course, empathy involves a lot of risks. In this society, with its frontier tradition and its emphasis on competition, it is often seen quite literally as a liability. How much of a favor do you do a son, in particular, when you teach him to be gentle? Even to be a gentleman?

The real world — the world of lane-changers on the freeway, of brutal competition, of human struggle and international conflict — comes crashing in. The gentle can become the vulnerable; civility can be seen as weakness or uncertainty about goals.

I remember the disdain a friend of mine used to express for Jimmy Carter — "the Sunday school teacher from Plains," he would say with a voice dripping with contempt. He wanted his leaders as much schooled in the teaching of "The Prince" as in the Sermon on the Mount.

I think I understand that. There is a need for decisiveness in a leader, a need that Jimmy Carter often failed to meet. The effective leader sometimes has to be ruthless in choosing the lesser among evils. Machiavelli was at least partly right about the art of statecraft.

Compassion is not much in vogue these days. Even common courtesy and mutual respect sometimes seem to be liabilities rather than assets.

Still, it seemed a wonderful little triumph when this one little boy thought first not of himself but of his sister.

It won't redeem the world.

The pattern in that one incident won't even necessarily be repeated the next time she has a cookie and he wants it.

Forgive me, though, for hoping it means something.

When your child becomes an adult

She did not come home this Easter, but I felt very close to her nonetheless.

Her spring break this year was consumed by interviews for summer jobs in St. Louis and Chicago and the mad dash up the middle of the country from New Orleans required to make all of this fall into place.

She could easily have felt that her father and the rest of her family were hovering, barely off the stage, trying to provide long-distance guidance and protection. She is, after all, 21, and she has traveled before without benefit of parental supervision. A little chafing would have been understandable. If she felt any of that, though, she never betrayed it.

Instead, she seemed pumped up by this rite of passage. I have a vision of her in the cab in St. Louis, heading for the first of the interviews, with her architectural portfolio in hand. When I finally caught up with her by phone at Grandmother's house on the way back to school, she was kind enough and open enough to share the details. I relished it.

The details matter mostly to her and, vicariously, to those who love her. What is more universal is the sense I had of the splendid tension between wanting to be supportive and wanting to stay out of the way, the sense of pride in and love for a young woman beginning to try her wings and stake her claim on life. Fatherhood has its moments. The past week provided a lot of them even though she was there, and I was here.

MARCH 26, 1989

The loving child of 5 becomes soon the perverse teenager of 15. But then, if you're very lucky, there comes a moment when they become adults and stand toe-to-toe with you as adults.

It's odd sometimes, the things that you remember about relationships. Our memories hang on little snippets of scenes: I can remember standing at the car door, saying good-bye to my father, leaving to go back to grad school. I wanted to embrace him. Instead, I shook his hand. He would have thought it awkward and odd, but I wish I had embraced him.

The passages from childhood to adolescence to adulthood are often complex and full of pain as well as joy. The loving child of 5 becomes soon the perverse teenager of 15. But then, if you're very lucky, there comes a moment when they become adults and stand toe-to-toe with you as adults. If you're very lucky indeed, you may even provide more help than hurt as they try to negotiate that transition.

Then they become separate from you, with their own styles and interests and abilities. At that point, you watch with admiration and fear and hope. You can't really do much more, except to continue to love them.

Later on, there come other moments. You need a friend, and they're there. They need a friend, and you're there. You both manage to bring it off with a minimum of excess baggage. You even like each other. Those adult-to-adult relationships with your children can sometimes fill up a lot of lonely places in your heart.

We're a little closer to that now, she and I, after this week. She knew I wanted it all to work for her, and she accepted that. I knew she wanted to do it in her own way, and I accepted that. I can play all the little parent games in my head, and I will: What did she wear? What did she say? How did it go? You can never know, exactly. At some point, you know it's time to bite your tongue.

What you also know is that it was a wonderfully good feeling, watching her from afar, seeing the young woman she has become.

The child grows, but the values remain

During Holy Week, I find myself enveloped with memories of the small-town Methodist church in which I grew up: Of Aunt Gertrude in the choir, of the lilies on the altar, of the Easter hymns, of the beauty and hopefulness of the spring season.

And thinking of those things, I am drawn back not to particular dogmas, but to values that I grew up caring about: compassion and justice, integrity and tolerance, gentleness and strength. Through all the years that have intervened since I sat in that church and puzzled about the mysteries of life and wondered about the larger world outside that town, I have never felt any estrangement from that little boy and those values.

It was a good base — not a perfect base, perhaps; too shaped by race and class and ignorance and limitations and prejudice, perhaps. I have changed and learned and grown; I do not have to drive my father's Oldsmobile or to define myself or my philosophy of life or my faith precisely as my parents defined theirs. Life moves on, and so must we.

APRIL 15, 1990

We need to find the wisdom and the courage to provide some such base for our children: to stand for something, to help them identify a set of core values that will give a foundation for life.

But we need to be instructed by what they were and what we were, when we were their children and when the world beyond seemed so beautiful, so new, so threatening. Somehow we need to process those lessons we learned at their knees, to be reinforced by them and not paralyzed by them, to know ourselves and our roots, to be true to them and yet to be liberated by them.

And we need to find the wisdom and the courage to provide some such base for our children: to stand for something, to help them identify a set of core values that will give a foundation for life. We need to understand how much we do instruct them, whether we mean to do so or not.

Last Easter, I talked on Saturday about going to the sunrise service the next morning at the Methodist church. My 6-year-old wanted to get up and go with me, and she did. I thought at the time she was disappointed and puzzled by the service. The sun did not really rise in her presence; it was a small and rather dark chapel. She found much of the service obscure and incomprehensible. She sat on my lap part of the time and colored on the back of an offering envelope part of the time. I was afraid it was lost on her, perhaps even counterproductive.

Just last week, though, she looked at me with her wonderful brown eyes and asked me if we could go again this year. It was somehow important to her — as much for the companionship with me, I suspect, the sense of there being a very special quality to our relationship in the light of early morning, as for anything she understood about the words themselves or even the music. Still, I think she begins to understand a little of what it means.

I do celebrate those values these days. I yearn to transmit to my children a sense of composure and strength that can be battered and still go on. I wish for them that they could understand how sure it is that at some time in their lives they will walk through the valley of the shadow and how needy they will feel at that moment. I don't want to dictate to them the precise shape of their faith, or sense of self, or understanding of human nature. But I hope I can help them to come to adulthood whole, with a sense of integrity and both a sense of humility and a sense of being comfortable with themselves.

Life is not easy. It will have its share of pain for most of us. We will have to change and adapt and rethink our approach to life from time to time. We will make mistakes; we are capable of doing terribly wrong things. But if we can come to terms with ourselves and our roots and our possibilities, then maybe we can find a little joy along the way.

Values and roots do matter. Not my values and roots to the exclusion of or at the expense of yours necessarily. We do need to go back to who we were and who we are and what we hope our children will be. We do need the rich heritage that is ours and the wonderful possibilities that life itself gives us. We need to learn to be happy.

So Annie and I will go together through the early morning darkness and come home a little later in the early morning light. And maybe she will understand, as I think I do, that there is a faith and that there are values that matter a very great deal, that can help you to maintain your composure in the face of the terrors of the night when you are 7 or when you are 70. I hope it will help to give her strength for all that life can sometimes bring.

The best present can be a sense of self

She had been a teddy bear and an angel before, but now she had graduated to being a sugarplum, and it was clear we were entering a whole new phase with "The Nutcracker."

Practices were much more serious business now, and she endured the long waits with more patience and perspective than I would have expected from her. And when her sister brought her a corsage for the night of the first performance, she became sure that this and she were something very special.

And after her final performance on Saturday afternoon, she insisted that she and her mother go to another performance by another cast so she could enjoy the story from beginning to end. Afterward, she speculated about what role she could aspire to play next year and whether her parents just might find an Uncle Drosselmeyer doll to go with her Clara.

There is something very beautiful about watching her plunge into something she loves this much — something requiring a bit of commitment and discipline. Taking one last, lingering look at her asleep on her pillow, her golden hair still showing the benefits of the pre-performance care, I find myself thinking how much she has grown up this year. Some of the innocence has slipped away, but I enjoy seeing her personality evolve. The baby girl is becoming a whole person.

DEC. 23, 1990

I wish this gift for my children and for all children everywhere: Love yourselves, believe that life is a very special gift, know that the spark inside of you is almost unique and worth being nurtured by you and respected by others.

I hope she emerges, in the full flowering of her life, not just being a whole person, but knowing she is a special person. There's a risk of conceit in that, I suppose. It would be too bad if the sense of being special turned to vanity or self-absorption.

But it seems to me, as I struggle with life and with parenthood, that if I can give her the gift of believing she is a special being, of knowing who she is and what she values, I will have given her something very worthwhile.

Too many of us, having endured bone-chilling criticism from a parent or someone else, come to adulthood doubting ourselves, hating what we are, lacking the power to become what we could be. We struggle all our lives or at least until we're well along in years to arrive at self-acceptance. I am what I am, I can be better of course, but I can stand toe-to-toe with the world and know how, in Rudyard Kipling's phrase, "to walk with crowds and keep your virtue, or walk with kings nor lose the common touch."

It is certainly true, and it is said often enough, that many children today are sorely in need of discipline. They need to learn to accept no as an answer; they need to be challenged to take responsibility for themselves; they need to learn to wait. I find I always have to push myself to be demanding enough, so much did I yearn for my own father ever to say the encouraging word.

Still, I think it unlikely that we can ever really love them too much or believe in them too much. Indulge them too much? Of course we shouldn't. Surely, though, it is not a mistake to let them know how many possibilities you see in them and how much you care about them simply for what they are. It is a powerful lesson to learn that someone cares for you and that you don't have to struggle to earn that.

At this happy and holy season, with its emphasis on family and joy and peace, I wish this gift for my children and for all children everywhere: Love yourselves, believe that life is a very special gift, know that the spark inside of you is almost unique and worth being nurtured by you and respected by others.

Life even at this ostensibly happy season always has a bittersweet quality. Life is not easy.

But life is a gift, and if life gives you the chance to be a sugarplum, be the best sugarplum you can be.

Life will have enough surprises to save you from conceit.

What you have to hope, when the hard times come, is that from somewhere in the programming that we get from childhood, there is a small voice that tells us we really are and can always be a very special sugarplum indeed.

Uncle Joe brought a gift of adventure

When she called to report about Uncle Joe's being in the hospital, it was hard not to figure that, well, this is it.

He is, after all, 93, and her voice had an edge to it as she talked about how determined she was to find a way to go from South Arkansas down to South Texas to see him.

A few days later, she called back to say that he was rallying from the heart valve leakage problem, was at home again in Seguin, and was weak but on his way back to being his wonderful puckish self. He was not ready to check out quite yet, thank you.

Every family needs an Uncle Joe. I was named after him, and on those infrequent occasions when he would show up at our farm, having come from some exotic place, he made me think that there were places out there that I wanted to see. The knickknack shelves in the farmhouse were laden with mementos of his travels, from Brazil and Ecuador, a fork taken from a German U-boat captured in World War I.

MARCH 24, 1991

Though I seldom saw Uncle Joe more than once or twice a year at best, he has been a powerful presence in my life. His life said to me, as a farm boy bound to evening chores, that there is a wonderful world out there.

He was an old Navy man, a communications expert whose career spanned both world wars and Korea, who had been with radio through the early days, and who kept his mind and his skills sharp over a remarkable span of years. He had run away from home to join the Navy back when this century was still relatively young and war was coming on, fibbing about his age to move on to a larger world than that defined by his Baptist preacher father. And even as late as the '60s, he would still occasionally get bored, sidle on down to Galveston or some other port, and ship out on a tanker bound for the Persian Gulf.

Uncle Joe was a restless soul, and he never ceased to love the world of sea and ships and freedom. I'm sure there are times even now, down at his retirement home in Seguin, when the wind brings with it a certain smell of adventure and the old yearning to go to sea comes back again, and Joe McKinney wishes he were young enough to push out to sea once more.

On his rare visits back to his native Arkansas to see his baby sister, his iconoclasm would pierce the ashen skies of well-set moralism like a thunderbolt. He would tease his baby sister — his earnest, moralistic baby sister — and she would warm to his jaunty games-playing even when she missed the joke. She, too, drew vicarious satisfaction from his worldliness and his wit and his ability to laugh at himself and at everything around him.

Maybe it was illusion, but Uncle Joe always seemed a risk-taker in a family of caution and commitment. The rest of us might show up every day at 9-to-5 desk jobs, but not Uncle Joe. He was and is someone who had kept on, year after year, going out to meet life. Even a phone conversation with him could be an adventure. You never were quite sure where his iconoclasm would take him. You could safely say only that he would be different.

I have seldom visited an exotic place in the world — Rio or Guayaquil or the Cape of Good Hope and Victoria Falls — without thinking, at least fleetingly, of Uncle Joe and his wanderlust. My dad was so set in his ways, so bound to his sense of place, that he would not take a job in a town an hour away from where he grew up because he thought it was better to live "where people know you." Dad was the very essence of the "reasonably prudent man." I had a strong sense of my roots in that Arkansas soil, too, and a sense of responsibility that is both a curse and a blessing. Still, something there was that didn't love the walls of that world.

A few years ago, standing in the blowing mist at the lookout above the Cape, I understood how the likes of Uncle Joe could love the pull of the sea so much — the sense of being connected to the world, to all sorts of possibilities and all sorts of sights to be seen. Though I seldom saw him more than once or twice a year at best, he has been a powerful presence in my life. His life said to me, as a farm boy bound to evening chores, that there is a wonderful world out there. And now, as a man, I am not surprised to find that, having brushed against death, he decided that he still had some living to do, even at 93.

Uncle Joe always did march to his own special cadence, and there was surely no reason to believe it would be any different now, when it was a different kind of sea that was calling.

A steel magnolia looks back, moves on

At her age, and with all that is happening over the next month, you would expect her to be looking back.

She is, after all, almost 86, and at the end of this month she will be saying good-bye to a corner of the world that has been home since 1924. She will leave the house in town that she and my late father bought together 19 years ago, and there will be no member of our family living in that community for the first time in more than 100 years.

And she is looking back. One of her friends put together a coffee for her, and 150 women showed up to say good-bye. The library board will have a reception later this month. The historical society is wondering who will continue to maintain the light that she has provided on the town's past. She taught school a generation ago, and a Sunday school class for a decade, and there are still those around who care about Miz Stroud.

SEPT. 22, 1991

She will go in as she always has, with her eyes front and her opinions intact and the hope that somehow she will find the strength to deal with what life brings.

The business of selling the house and parceling out the mementos of a lifetime makes the rest of us look back, too. She wanted me to have the rolltop desk that was her father's, given to him, she remembers, by a turn-of-the-century governor of Arkansas. The cabinets' being gradually emptied of papers and pictures brings back those years when she provided order and sustenance in what could have been and sometimes was a stark, male-dominated household. She really was and is a steel magnolia, you understand, as you sift through those memories.

She had come to that country, those dreary, swampy flatlands, at a time when it was a very hard struggle with dirt and heat and flood and ignorance. She had valued education before most folks understood its importance. She had taught English to hulking farm boys already twice her size. In the years before electricity and running water and telephones, she had fought to keep her sons clean and to protect them from the diseases that thrived in the summer heat. She had insisted on baths when it meant filling washtubs and corralling growing boys to scrub behind their ears.

Always, she had valued learning. She collected what books she could, and used what library there was, and never believed her sons should be intimidated by the hard world lying up the road beyond the county line or even the borders of Arkansas. As the family crawled out of the Great Depression, she worked hard to help them believe that all things were possible, that they need not spend their whole lives huddled close around her skirts.

That approach to life had its price. Each of the sons wound up eventually working for big-city newspapers, not tending the farm or working in the bank. No one stayed home to help guarantee that she could manage on her own. But she managed pretty well on her own, thriving after her husband's death and recovering after her own stroke, stubbornly refusing to surrender her independence and her privacy. She managed to make do with phone calls and letters and photographs of the grandchildren and great-grandchildren. She was thrilled when one of her granddaughters managed the feat of delivering a son — her only great-grandson — precisely on Mamaw's birthday.

So, yes, she is looking back. But if all goes according to plan, she will close up that house in the early part of October, have the mover pack her scaled-down possessions off to St. Louis, and be herself driven off to Little Rock for the flight to St. Louis and her new apartment near where the oldest son lives. She will shed some more tears as she goes, but she will be ready to stop looking back.

From what she says to me on the phone, she will go out with good cheer and strong hopes, ready to try to adapt again to city life and for the first time ever to a small apartment instead of a house, and to a small balcony instead of a grassy yard. She will go in as she always has, with her eyes front and her opinions intact and the hope that somehow she will find the strength to deal with what life brings.

Steel magnolias can be frustrating sometimes. She still sniffs at the idea of riding in a van to go to church or do her grocery shopping. And you can only whisper a silent prayer that she will be tolerant enough of new people and new routines. Life has been hard and sometimes disappointing for her before, though she has had her share of life's blessings, too. She has met it all, mostly with strength and grace, and she will meet this, too.

As she goes on to this phase in her life, her sons will know that they are very, very lucky to have her as a compass, as a guidebook to how to deal with life as it comes, treating triumph and disaster for the impostors that they really are. They will savor the memory, as she does, of what her life in that community has been and look ahead, as she does, to whatever it is that life may put next on the agenda.

An act of concern lights up the season

She danced across the kitchen, clutching in her hands a fetching poster of a kitten. Her book order had arrived at school, and with it the new poster for the wall in her bedroom.

I admired it, and we talked about whether it looked like her kitten, Stuf (as in Double Stuf Oreo cookies), and she glowed with pleasure at her acquisition. She was thankful for the wall hanging.

Then, without guile or smugness or regret or anything I could detect other than pure concern for someone else, she added: "I really got two with my book order, but Angelo didn't get anything, and I gave him the other poster."

I could scarcely contain my own pleasure and joy and pride in that little 8-year-old girl with the warm brown eyes and the golden hair. Somehow, almost instinctively, she understood the other side of thankfulness: to be able to walk in someone else's shoes, to be sensitive to someone else's need or feelings.

DEC. 1, 1991

I might struggle to help her learn reading, but she managed, with no effort at all, to teach me something about kindness and human connections.

That beautiful little moment, I thought, almost redeemed this wretched fall, with its harsh clash of ideologies, with so much being said and done that is mean-spirited and chilling. I had found strength and help in her before. I might struggle to help her learn reading, but she managed, with no effort at all, to teach me something about kindness and human connections.

But, my Lord, how we needed that lesson this fall. In her uncomplicated and straightforward response to her classmate's empty hand, she had provided a balm for the grief I have felt as I've tried to struggle with the ugly realities of this year.

It's not a new lesson for anyone about the spirit of this season and the holidays to follow. Many charities, like many department stores, either make it or don't on what they get around Thanksgiving and Christmas. People who scarcely think of charity at other times will put a copper in the Salvation Army kettle or a can or ham in the food basket for the poor.

This holiday season, though, surely those of us lucky enough to be working have to think about a little something beyond ourselves, beyond the usual. Blame whomever you will. Rage at Coleman Young, or John Engler, or George Bush, or Jimmy Carter, or Henry Ford, or whomever. Rage at me or anyone else who professes to care about this community and who has not succeeded at heading off some of the social and economic calamities we face this fall.

Argue for the restoration of the old-time liberal religion or the installation of the new-time neoconservative gospel if you will. Tell me it's all because we've forgotten God or because we've made gods who stole our compassion or good sense.

But don't tell me that you can walk or drive through the streets of this city and not grieve for the hardships and the anger and the dislocation that exist. Don't tell me that this city is not facing grievous danger this winter. Don't tell me that we can just walk away from what is happening in these streets.

I can't. I couldn't look into those beautiful brown eyes and rejoice at her act of concern for the feelings of her classmate anymore if I did. I couldn't tell her children, if and when she has children, that I did not recognize what a mess we faced this winter and that we had to try to mitigate what was happening.

At this season, I have been trying to catch my breath, trying to remember what Thanksgiving really means, trying to put the wrenching adjustments of this year into perspective.

Looking into those eyes, accepting her embrace at bedtime and in the morning, I think I've got the perspective I need to see me through.

Yes, I really am thankful.

Especially I am thankful for a little girl who knows how to care and who sometimes manages to teach her father.